4|19

WITHDR KT-419-629

Books should be returned or renewed by the last
date above. Renew by phone **03000 41 31 31** or
online *www.kent.gov.uk/libs*

About the author

Clare Gogerty is a journalist and award-winning magazine editor with an interest in pilgrimage, paths and prehistory. A career in print journalism has allowed her to indulge her passions and taken her off on many adventures. She has written about her travels for *Coast* magazine (which she edited for six years), the *Guardian* and *Conde Nast Traveller*, among many other publications. She is also the author of the *National Trust's Book of the Coast* and several National Trust coastal guidebooks. She continues to explore ancient sites at every opportunity and combines this with an enthusiasm for folklore, gardening and druidry.

CLARE
GOGERTY

BEYOND
THE
FOOTPATH

MINDFUL ADVENTURES
FOR MODERN PILGRIMS

piatkus

PIATKUS

First published in Great Britain in 2019 by Piatkus

1 3 5 7 9 10 8 6 4 2

Copyright © 2019 Clare Gogerty

A CIP catalogue record for this book
is available from the British Library.

Illustrations © Ruth Craddock

ISBN 978-0-349-41967-1

Typeset in Swift by M Rules
Printed and bound in Great Britain by
Clays Ltd, Elcograf S.p.A.

Papers used by Piatkus are from well-managed forests
and other responsible sources.

Piatkus
An imprint of
Little, Brown Book Group
Carmelite House
50 Victoria Embankment
London EC4Y 0DZ

An Hachette UK Company
www.hachette.co.uk

www.improvementzone.co.uk

To Mollie Gogerty, who took me to Walsingham –
my first pilgrimage – and has been with me
every step of the way since.

Contents

Contents

At the Threshold

Why go on a pilgrimage? I go to step out of my daily life for a few days – to follow a path that promises magic, beauty and surprise. It is a way of travelling from the humdrum concerns of the everyday, through a landscape that inspires, to a place of meaning. I leave behind the elbow tug of incessant news feeds, the struggle of daily commuting and the not-so-simple business of just keeping going. Instead of battling through crowds and watching cancellations on stations' departure boards, I can walk through forests or along the path of a river. Even in a city, it is possible to leave behind ordinary life for a while and go in search of the sacred.

With an alert mind and a bounce in my step, I am ready for whatever the pilgrimage may bring. And it always brings something, whether it's a personal insight, a creative idea, a greater connection with the natural world or my fellow human beings, or simply a day or two of uncomplicated living. A pilgrimage offers more than a long walk. A pilgrim is not a tourist. Pilgrimage has a deeper, more spiritual significance. It is simple and honest, and it delivers in unexpected ways.

The modern pilgrim

All over the world, people are going on pilgrimage. Boots are being pulled on, rucksacks packed and maps scrutinised as routes are planned. Pilgrimage is one of the fastest-growing movements in the world. According to the UN World Tourism Organisation, over 330 million people go on a pilgrimage every year. Even countries where pilgrimage has been in constant practice over the centuries have seen numbers swelling: over 30 million pilgrims went to the Hindu pilgrimage Maha Kumbh Mela in India on one day in 2013, and two million attend the Hajj in the holy city of Mecca every year.

The jump in numbers has been most noticeable on the Camino de Santiago in Spain. Once a route only walked by dedicated Catholics, it is now on the bucket list of many non-believers. Back in 1986, 2491 pilgrims completed the final 100-km stretch of the Camino, but by 2017, the figure had jumped to over 300,000.

While some still walk with religious intent – to ask for a prayer to be answered, as an act of penance or as a simple act of worship – other secular pilgrims take to the path for reasons of their own. They may have no religious faith at all but still be searching for something. This could simply be a new, enriching experience or something more profound. Finding themselves at a crossroads in their life, perhaps, they could be seeking a new direction and a purpose.

Modern pilgrims have found that the simple business of reaching a special place by putting one foot in front of the other provides what they are looking for. It's a way of connecting with something 'other', something spiritual. Walking a path is a slow and deliberate undertaking and can't be hurried. It offers what modern life is short of: time. It's a chance to press the pause button, give your mind a rest, and to look around. Pilgrimage today is more flexible than it has ever been. There is a pilgrimage for everyone, as this book will show. All you have to do is step out of your front door and walk.

A little history

When we hear the word 'pilgrim', most of us think in terms of the medieval Christian world. Whereas this might cramp our understanding of what pilgrimage can mean today, knowing a little about its history does help to place it, and provides a link with fellow pilgrims from the past.

Pilgrimages have been a common feature of most world religions for as long as they have existed. Buddhism, Jainism, Islam, Judaism, Hinduism and Shinto all place it at the core of their religious practice. The golden age of Christian pilgrimages was the Middle Ages, peaking in the twelfth century, when most Christians were impelled to visit a significant site, preferably one that housed the bones of a saint or some other relic, or a tomb of a martyr. Getting close to these artefacts, and to the actual bodies, of the holy was thought to bring you closer to God, make your prayers more powerful and bring healing. Pilgrims would touch and kiss these relics, if possible, for maximum impact. Even better, they took some part away with them: at Canterbury Cathedral the blood and brains of Thomas Becket, spilt during his murder, were endlessly diluted with water to sell to pilgrims.

The three main pilgrimage destinations were Rome, Jerusalem and Santiago de Compostela, and reaching them was a risky and lengthy business. Some richer Christians even paid others to walk in their stead. Pilgrimage was not for the faint-hearted: on the longer routes illness, robbery and even murder were frequent. As a sort of insurance policy, before setting off, pilgrims attended Mass where a priest blessed their belongings and said prayers. To keep them safe, they would carry staffs which, as well as helping them walk, kept menacing animals (and marauders) at bay, and could be used to clear paths of foliage. Pilgrims travelled light. They took a leather pouch or slim satchel to carry bread and any necessary documents, and wore a broad-brimmed hat (turned up at the front to display a scallop shell if Santiago was the destination), a tunic and a cloak. These items were the emblems of a pilgrim – the scallop shell is still worn by modern pilgrims as they walk the Camino towards Santiago de Compostela.

A pilgrimage was a great leveller: everyone from kings to pig farmers took to the road (as illustrated by the disparate characters chronicled in Chaucer's *Canterbury Tales*). Some pilgrimages were undertaken as a penance for a sin, with pilgrims choosing to walk barefoot – some on their knees as they neared the shrine, others even in shackles. It was thought that the pilgrimage was purified by the pain and effort spent in getting there.

Unlike modern times, when walking is a pleasurable choice, in the Middle Ages it was the only way to travel – apart from horseback – and the difficulty it presented was part of the point of pilgrimage. For some, a pilgrimage was the only journey they ever made, and the only time they left their own village or town.

The mass movement of pilgrims across Europe ended at the Reformation, and pilgrimage was banned by Henry VIII and Thomas Cromwell. All the old paths lay unwalked until the twentieth century, from which time they were gradually rediscovered and trod once more. These included not just the big routes to major destinations, like Santiago de Compostela, but also smaller, more local paths to prehistoric sites, ancient churches, holy wells, waterfalls, hills and anywhere else considered sacred or significant.

Now the revival of pilgrimage is seeing a new merry band take to the road – one with modern sensibilities and hi-tech outdoor clothing, a variety of destinations and motivations propelling them onward.

The power of pilgrimage

Although there's no denying that walking a long distance can be demanding – there will be blisters to deal with, fatigue to overcome, and unexpected obstacles to get around – these difficulties are easier to manage if considered part of the experience. If the walking was all ease and comfort, there would be no sense of achievement at the end, and little spirit of adventure. You might as well do the journey in an overheated coach and barely give the road a glance through the window as you motor past. Besides, any discomfort or inconvenience is eclipsed by the magic of the road. The unfolding landscape, the steady tread of your footsteps, the discovery of sacred places and a general sense of wellbeing – happiness even – that rises from your feet to your heart more than compensate for the pinching of an uncomfortable boot or a sunburnt nose. Here are some of the benefits I've learnt to appreciate.

You feel the magic of a place

Every so often you come across a place that immediately seems special: it has a magic all of its own, so much so that it makes you feel more alive and you don't want to leave. This can happen accidentally in daily life by stumbling across a secret garden in a busy city, say, or popping into a church out of curiosity one lunchtime and finding it to be a place of serenity and holiness. But it's more likely to happen on a pilgrimage.

The pilgrim's mind is open and responsive; it is drawn to the numinous, whether that spiritual quality inhabits a man-made monument or a place of natural beauty. Among the places where I have tuned into the *genus loci*, or spirit of a place, are an ancient woodland in North London, a stone circle overlooking a bay in Ireland, a well on a Scottish island and a car park on Exmoor. As Philip Carr-Gomm writes in *The Druid Way* (a book about a pilgrimage across the South Downs): 'All we have to do is enter it in the right spirit and the landscape will begin to speak to us.'

Life becomes simple

Shutting the door behind you and setting out on foot early in the morning with just a rucksack on your back is powerful and liberating. Going for a long walk necessitates paring back the clutter of life to the bare minimum. You leave behind all the stuff that surrounds you every day, all those things that need managing, cleaning and repairing, and take only what you need to keep you going.

Carrying everything you need on your back simplifies choice. Suddenly that extra pair of shoes doesn't seem so necessary. Unlike conventional holidays with their many wardrobe options (What shall I pack for the evening? Do I need a jumper if it gets cold? Should I pack a waterproof?), all you need to take on a pilgrimage are the essentials. A good pair of boots, a change of socks and underwear, lightweight clothing that you can handwash, a bottle of water and your phone should do it. (This is the most minimal list: there are a few supplementary suggestions on page 221.)

Decisions vanish too. All you have to do is keep putting one foot in front of the other and head in the right direction. Some pilgrimage routes are clearly waymarked, so map-reading options are also taken care of (although it's a good idea to carry a map as a back-up), or you may choose to go with an organised group and leave navigation to the leader. With all the aggravating and tiresome aspects of life left behind, all you have to concentrate on is the simple task of keeping walking.

You give your mind a rest

Concentrating on the path, thinking about where to put your feet if you are scrambling down a mountain, or how to cross a stream without falling in, helps to create a meditative state. The monkey chatter of the mind is silenced as you pay attention to staying upright and not breaking an ankle. This leaves the mind clear for other more radical thoughts to pop up. Walking artist Hamish Fulton points out that: 'You stop the endless thinking mind. And that's a good thing – because every now and then you want to stop going down the same neural pathways. Then you have other perceptions.'

You journey inwards as well as outwards

The urge to go on pilgrimage has always been with us: evidence of people travelling to sacred places goes back to prehistoric times. It is embedded in the human psyche and not just as a way to worship, but as a personal need, a psychological necessity. The call to leave home and go on a journey of discovery comes to everyone, but we don't all choose to hear it. Those that do, learn that a pilgrimage is a way to find themselves, to consider who they are and where they are on their path through life. Pilgrimage is often compared to life's journey from birth to death, with the promise of redemption and/or rebirth at the end.

It is also an opportunity to reconnect our inner selves with our bodies and the external world. Too often we live entirely in our heads, preoccupied with thinking about the stresses of everyday life, regretting the past, fearing or anticipating the future. We neglect our bodies, take them for granted, and reduce them to mere vehicles for getting us about, or for containing our minds.

On pilgrimage we become aware of our bodies once more. We feel the ache in our muscles and the power of our feet. We sense our legs getting stronger, our hearts beating and our lungs working. As pilgrimage marries our inner journey with our outer one, it awakens the body once more and unites it with the mind.

You learn things

You'll gain awareness, not just about your surroundings and the places you visit, but also about yourself. The road is a great teacher. Who knew you could walk so far? Or that you had the determination to carry on when a little voice inside urged you to get the train home? Of course, you could learn less positive things about yourself, too, but that's a risk worth taking.

You also learn from those you meet on your way, whether they are fellow pilgrims or people encountered more fleetingly along the path. These chance encounters bring you in contact with those you would not otherwise have met. They will tell you their stories, share information and even teach you things about yourself.

You re-energise old paths

Walking ancient trackways and routes not only prevents them from becoming overgrown and vanishing but brings them back to life. The Gatekeeper Trust, an organisation 'devoted to personal and planetary healing through pilgrimage', believes that the earth can be turned into light through pilgrimage. They quote an old saying that every pilgrim leaves footprints of light (in my mind, like Michael Jackson in the 'Billie Jean' video, illuminating paving slabs with each step) so that others may follow and then add their own. This positive energy then radiates to the surrounding environment and lights that too.

Ways to go – approaching a pilgrimage

The power of a pilgrimage lies in its simplicity. The only danger is to overthink it or to expect too much. Approach your pilgrimage with a light and open heart, and surprising things will occur.

Like all journeys, a pilgrimage has a beginning, a middle and an end. Each has a different significance and will have a different impact on your thinking and emotions. Be aware of how you respond to each part: how you feel at the start of your walk compared to how you feel when you have finished. Be conscious of the fluctuations of sensations and moods that occur in the middle, but don't try to change how you feel – accept these emotions and keep walking.

As you walk, use all five senses

Listen to the silence. Is it pure or is it made up of many small noises: the crunch of your footsteps, a twig breaking beneath your boots, a bird flying from a tree, the distant hum of traffic? If you walk through snow, the silence will feel different, softer, deeper, muffled. If it rains, put on your waterproof and enjoy the sound it makes driving onto the road, or dripping from branches.

Inhale and smell the air. In a forest, breathe the pine-scented air, damp wood, wet leaves. By the sea, the air smells clean, seaweedy, salty. On open moorland, sniff the coconut smell of gorse, the heather, damp sheep. In cities, you may smell the unexpected aroma of orange blossom (Seville in spring), grass freshly mown in a park, bread baking at a supermarket door or coffee beans being roasted in a café.

Feel the ground beneath your feet. Is it hard or is it yield-ing? Try taking your boots off and walking barefoot. It is soothing to walk on dew-laden grass, sun-warmed mud or the cool, hard sand of the strandline. Instead of walking past, stop for a moment and touch a tree and feel its gnarled bark, or dip your fingers in a stream and feel its crisp vitality.

Look all around you, not just at the path in front. You are in no hurry, there's plenty of time to watch the clouds build on the horizon or to follow the movement of a wave from the ocean to the shore. Take time to look closely, too: observe a flower, leaf or shell closely and notice its colours, patterns and structure.

Taste the sea air on your lips, the sweetness of a wild straw-berry or a ripe blackberry plucked from a bush. Even a humble sandwich tastes better when it's eaten outdoors.

Let the muse settle on your shoulder

You may find that as you walk, unexpected ideas and thoughts come to mind. Let words find you. Stop by the wayside when they do and jot them down. (A notebook with an all-weather cover is best!) As you travel, you may hear of stories and myths that you want to record, or you may be inspired to invent some of your own.

Or you could see something remarkable that you want to capture. A snap on the phone will do it, but a pencil drawing will slow you down and make you really look at your subject, studying it closely. A sketch will also have more meaning because it will have some part of you embedded within it.

And when you get to the end

Different emotions surface at the end of a pilgrimage. While a pilgrimage is not about conquering anything, a fitness challenge, or a stab at some sort of notoriety, completing one is, nevertheless, an achievement to be proud of and to take pleasure from. When the walking is over, however, a feeling of anti-climax and 'what now?' sometimes settles on the pilgrim. The only road ahead now is the one that takes you back home to normal life and daily routine. Be prepared for this by cherishing what you have experienced on your travels.

The British Pilgrimage Trust suggest that, as at the end of life, when we relinquish our bodies, we should let go of something treasured at the end of a pilgrimage. They recommend throwing away a pilgrim's staff into a stream or the sea with a breezy cheerio. If you don't carry a staff, you could try releasing something else that has been important to you during the pilgrimage: a water bottle or a pair of socks (but dispose of them thoughtfully into a recycling bin rather than chuck them into a stream!). A carefree approach to the final steps of your pilgrimage will ease you back into regular life. And besides, it won't be long before you are planning your next pilgrimage and will be back on the footpath again.

A mindful pilgrimage

Mindfulness has become a word of our times, with more and more of us using techniques to live in the moment and accept, then release, thoughts and feelings. Although the origins of mindfulness lie in Buddhism, we can adopt it whatever our beliefs, applying it to whatever we are doing. In Buddhism, mindfulness is the seventh element of the Eightfold Path and necessitates attentiveness, alertness and awareness. If we mentally occupy these three states, Buddhists believe that we avoid sleepwalking through life and instead wake up to its possibilities.

Mindful walking is especially effective because the steady and rhythmic act of putting one foot in front of the other stills the mind and focuses thoughts on the path instead. As we walk, our bodies come alive, our hearts pump, lungs inflate and deflate, and our heads clear. We are refreshed and invigorated. It is one of our simplest actions, and one of the most effective.

There are times on your pilgrimage when you will want to behave 'normally' – chat to others, let your thoughts drift, stop and eat an ice cream or stroke a horse's nose. Walk with a mindful approach for sections of the walk, though, and you will feel the benefits, mentally and spiritually. Thoughts will rise as the path opens in front of you, and you will get a taste of the giddiness that comes with the freedom of the road.

Here is a general guide to help with your mindful walking practice. There are other exercises throughout the book.

- Turn off your phone.
- Make an intention.
- Engage all senses.
- Walk slowly but purposefully, trying to maintain a regular, steady pace.
- Look up. Look around. Every so often, look behind to reflect on how far you've come.

- Breathe slowly and deeply.
- Learn the names of what you see – trees, butterflies, wild flowers – it's a way of noticing.
- Keep a journal but don't let it dominate. A few jottings will do. Noting things helps you pay attention to what is around you.
- Dismiss any annoying or upsetting thoughts. Concentrate on the here and now.
- Every so often, stand still.
- Be quiet. Engaging with others is a distraction, so give it a break – at least for a while. Or walk with a close friend in companiable silence.
- Give a cheery hello to strangers you meet on the path.
- Just walk.

1

Ancient Paths

Walking in the footsteps of our ancestors gives
us a real sense of the path's past and of the
people who walked it centuries ago.

I had driven through Dartmoor on my way to Cornwall many
times. I had itched to stop and explore it, but had always been
in too much of a hurry. There were usually B&Bs to get to, or
a chip shop to reach before it closed. As I drove towards the
chosen holiday destination, Dartmoor would roll on around
me, filling the windscreen with its open moorland, peculiar
rock formations and wild ponies. It looked like a place you
could get lost in easily and never be found. Somewhere you
could walk for ages and not see a soul. Somewhere to clear the
head and open the heart. It was also, I knew, bristling with
prehistoric sites, including seventy (the largest concentration

in Britain) of those intriguing Neolithic pathways: stone rows. I made a note to myself to return to see them, to go on a pilgrimage to find a stone row or two, and to see if I could walk with the ancients.

Stone rows comprise two lines of standing stones (although some have three) that lead in a vaguely straight path to a stone circle or a cist (grave). Kennet Avenue at Avebury (see page 151) is a fine example of a procession way lined with stone rows, taking the pilgrim along a sacred path from The Sanctuary hillside to Avebury henge. Dartmoor is the place to head to see a multitude of stone rows of various sizes and directions, as well as many other Neolithic and Bronze Age monuments.

I was keen to set my boots in the very same places that my ancestors had walked, and to experience a little of what they had experienced, so when I heard that author and 'stone seeker' Peter Knight was running a Dartmoor Mindscapes Weekend with his partner, Sue Wallace – the object of which was to 'connect on a deeper level with this magical landscape' – I signed up and persuaded my friend Carolyn to come along. Peter and Sue have spent a great deal of time on Dartmoor, clambering up tors, pacing around stone circles and generally responding to and trying to make sense of what they see and experience. Sometimes their activities are shamanic, and drum beating, chanting and the reading of poetry are involved.

Peter is convinced that the domination of the landscape by sizeable and distinctively shaped granite tors meant that prehistoric peoples considered them to be sacred in their own right. Many tors resemble figures (famously Bowerman's Nose, which has the profile of a giant) and animals (we came across one shaped exactly like a bear), so this is entirely feasible. These 'simulacra', he reckons, may have inspired the ancients to create their own stone monuments, either as a response or to connect with them in some way.

Simulacra are not just confined to Dartmoor: they are recognised, and have been worshipped, by people worldwide, from Egypt to Australia. It seems that the human mind is programmed to look for faces and figures on mountains, in rocks and on cliff faces – be they gods or animals.

We spent the first day looking for faces in boulders, rocking on balancing stones (and tapping some to listen to their sonorous tone – these musical stones are known as lithophones) and dipping our fingers into rainwater collected in circular rock basins. Carolyn, who has spent time with shamans in Hawaii and travelled widely in the Far East, was struck by the similarity of some of the tors to stupa on Buddhist temples in Myanmar. As we walked in silent meditation towards Great Staple Tor, its towering piles of rocks silhouetted dramatically against a bright blue sky, it did indeed feel as though we were approaching a temple. It must have felt similarly awe-inspiring to the Neolithic people of Dartmoor.

We spent time exploring the Merrivale ceremonial landscape later that afternoon. I walked along my first stone row and we spent a while dowsing for earth energies around a stone circle (see page 26), but it was the next day I anticipated the most. Merrivale is packed with interest and well worth a visit, but it's near a road and a car park, and takes little effort to reach. Brisworthy stone circle, and Ringmoor cairn circle and stone row, the next day's destinations, were more remote: we would have to leave our cars and go on foot to reach them.

The walk to Brisworthy took us along hedgerow-lined paths and over fields decorated with cow pats. It was a hot summer's day and the countryside hummed with insects. The approach to a sacred place always fills me with a mixture of curiosity, solemnity and anticipation. I can't wait to see it, but I don't want to hurry to find it, and the moment it reveals itself is always a thrill.

The tops of the Brisworthy stones appeared above a gentle swell in the landscape, and then, as we drew closer, there was the entire thing – a series of stumpy stones graduated in size towards the south – tucked into a north-facing slope overlooking the Plym Valley.

We all took time to walk around the circle and choose a stone to sit by. All the talking and exclamations stopped as we settled down to meditate. Peter had said that the surrounding landscape, with its great tors on hill summits and views of the sea (now obscured by the spoils from a china clay quarry), had played an important part in the siting of the circle. Although Dartmoor today is open moorland, it is very likely that during the Late Neolithic period, and possibly into the Bronze Age, it was largely forested. The circles and rows were probably constructed at the forest edge to allow for sightlines of landmarks. I thought about that for a while, and how modern buildings are constructed with little thought for where the sun rises, never mind how they relate to the natural topography. Then I let my mind settle and simply enjoyed sitting there.

Reflections over, we headed away from the circle, further up the slope and on to Ringmoor itself. Peter pointed out that Steep Tor dipped beneath the skyline as we progressed, to reappear later. This would have been noticed by our forebears, he figured, and factored into the placement of the stones. It was also noted by poet Martin Shaw, who spent two years living in a yurt on Dartmoor: 'Landscape dances around us as we move,' he wrote. 'We don't travel over the land, rather with it.'

After a short walk of 300m, we reached a smaller circle with a cairn at its centre. Extending away from it, a position marked by a triangular stone, was the stone row I had been waiting for. The row was over 500m long and bent slightly to the north. Some stretches had double stones, but many were missing. It was hard to tell if it had once consisted of two rows all the way or whether the instances of single rows were intended. We walked quietly along it, passing between the rows, keeping a reasonable distance between us, slowly being drawn out onto the moor. A straight line of reeds sprouted where the row petered out.

At the end of the row we turned and retraced our steps towards the cairn at the centre of the circle. It was the obvious thing to do: walking anywhere else wasn't an option. As Peter said, 'It feels as though our movements are being choreographed across the landscape.'

When I returned home, I read that archaeological investigations at Kennet Avenue in Avebury suggested that people had walked along the outside of the avenue and not between the rows of stones. That may have been true at Avebury, but on Ringmoor the stone row, which headed out across the rolling, expansive moorland towards distant tors and distinctive hills, then back towards the stone circle felt very much like a pathway, urging us pilgrims to walk along it and participate in something profound, just as our ancestors had before us.

Pilgrimages on ancient tracks

There is nothing like walking across a landscape to really get to know it. Drive past in a car and you'll get a glimpse, but it flashes past, the sighting transient and superficial. Tread over it a step at a time, though, and it slowly begins to reveal itself – not just the leaves and berries in the hedgerow or flowers in the meadow, but its spirit, its history and its people.

Nowhere is this truer than on an ancient track. Walking in the footsteps of our ancestors gives us a real sense of the path's past and of the people who walked it centuries ago. These old pathways existed before wheeled vehicles, when the only way to travel was on foot or by horseback. Despite the fact that many such routes have been obliterated over time by erosion and farming, or replaced by roads, traces of them still exist if you know where to look. Old pilgrim routes, especially those to and from sacred wells, churches and monastic settlements can be easy to find, although they may have become disguised over time.

Many old tracks survive on higher ground, where they have been untouched by modern development, and follow the undulations of south-facing slopes, sheltering travellers from the north wind. Some are old routes that connected ceremonial places used by priests and pilgrims, and others led to burial sites or simply to nearby villages. Along the way, landmarks such as distinctively shaped boulders and hills, fords, stone crosses and solitary trees provided navigational aids, helping travellers to get their bearings. Paths also diverted towards springs to refresh the weary, and to places that could provide rest and shelter. Continuing to walk these trackways keeps them alive. It is a collaborative process that involves our forebears, the land and ourselves. Without care and regular walking, paths simply disappear.

Paths across cultures and time

Ancient trackways hold different significances for different cultures. For the Celtic people in Britain, the paths themselves were thought to be sacred and protected by deities and spirits. Prayers or offerings were made to local holy beings to ensure a hazardless journey or to express gratitude for safely arriving. The Chinese practice of feng shui is based on the idea that natural forces manifest themselves as dragon lines, which run in straight lines. As spirits prefer to travel along the straightest routes, it is considered unlucky to build a house at the end of a straight road. In Ireland, legend has it that fairies, or the little people, had their own routes that ran between 'raths' (circular earthworks or forts) and it was unlucky to block them.

Aboriginal songlines: a summons to go walkabout

In Australia, the Aboriginal people still go on 'walkabouts' following the 'dreaming tracks' or 'songlines' laid down by their ancestors. The call to go on a long walk can come at any time. Once heard, everyday tasks are put aside and men and women begin to walk, following paths invisible and unknown by those around them.

According to their legends, when the world was being

created, ancestral beings in the shape of humans and animals emerged from its centre and wandered over the land, a period known as Alcheringa or the Dreaming. As they wandered, they conjured things into existence by singing the name of whatever they encountered. When Alcheringa ended, the ancestors themselves became mountains, caves, lakes and boulders – sacred sites such as Uluru and Kata Tjuta (see page 68).

The paths the ancestors walked, which connected these sacred places, have been followed by Aborigines for over four thousand years. As they follow these 'dreaming tracks', they sing songs about the ancestors that describe the location of landmarks on the route. By singing the songs in sequence, they travel vast distances. Some songlines are just a few kilometres long, others are hundreds. These songlines form a mesh of invisible tracks that cover Australia and must be sung to keep the land alive. Walking in this way enhances the natural energies that flow from the Earth's crust and is believed to help bring healing and balance to the environment and to the planet.

Native American pathways

Trails have always been an important part of Native American culture. They are the paths walked to bring in the harvest, to hunt, or to gather for rituals and celebrations. Thousands of miles of interconnecting trails crossed the American Southwest, from Texas to California to Mexico. They are scattered with artefacts – tools, pots, shrines, painted stones – that prove they were in constant use for millennia. Many of these treks were governed by the seasons: campsites were established in the desert for the agave harvest; on mountain slopes to gather nuts and juniper seeds; near a marsh to bag migratory water fowl; and near the plains to hunt buffalo.

Although most of these trails have vanished over time, you can see tracings of them at some river crossings and mountain passes. Further evidence of paths can be found by looking out for hardwood trees, like oak and maple, which have been intentionally bent into an upright L-shape several feet off the ground. These 'trail marker trees' are visible at great distances, even in the snow, and act as waymarkers to guide travellers towards their destinations.

The Chaco Culture National Historical Park in San Juan County, New Mexico, is the place to head to get a taste of the peripatetic life of the ancient Pueblo people. The buildings (now ruins) were a major sacred centre for them, and many structures were aligned according to the passage of the moon and the sun. A 400-mile network of roads radiates from Chaco Canyon in long, straight stretches – possibly used to distribute crops or, perhaps, as procession ways for pilgrims who followed them to join seasonal rituals and celebrations.

The old straight track: the mysterious world of ley lines

It's surprising that ley lines – a phenomenon that has taken on so many otherworldly connotations – was hatched by a sensible and pragmatic Herefordshire businessman. Alfred Watkins spent much of his working life driving along country roads on the way to appointments representing his family business. As he did so, he observed and photographed the landscape (he had a keen interest in photography). On 30 June 1921, on a road in Blackwardine near Leominster, he pulled up on a hillside when he noticed that a series of features – standing stones, wayside crosses, beacons, hill forts and ancient churches – were in alignment with one another 'like a chain of fairy lights'.

This experience kickstarted his theory that the entire landscape of Britain had once been crossed by intersecting straight lines that ran between prominent hills and other landmarks. These lines (called 'leys' because many of the places on the tracks had the Saxon suffix 'ley' or 'leigh', meaning forest clearing), he proposed, were either pathways used for traders carrying salt, pottery or flint, or had a ceremonial function. Following extensive travels and much photography, he published his findings in 1925 in *The Old Straight Track*, followed by *The Ley Hunter's Manual, a Guide to Early Tracks* in 1927.

Although discredited by archaeologists at the time, ley hunting quickly took off and became a popular pastime. To find a ley, Watkins suggested, you examine a map of the area (a scale of 1:50,000) and ring any features such as significant hills, standing stones, churches, prehistoric mounds, castles, fords and old tracks. Start with the most prominent site and look for others that line up with it. Draw a line between them and see if it extends to include others. As a guideline, five features within a 25-mile distance indicate that you are on to something. Having located your potential ley line, fieldwork is necessary: you might investigate further with a compass and proper scientific scrutiny.

Ley hunting fell out of favour with the outbreak of the

Second World War but was rekindled in the 1960s when the concept of leys was rediscovered by counterculture enthusiasts. Perhaps it is because ley lines are invisible and unprovable, but they became associated with all manner of supernatural activities, from UFOs to ancient astronomy and mystical energy lines. Ley hunters these days can be seen at ancient sites with dowsing rods looking for energy lines and astrological and geographical alignments.

One of the more interesting and convincing leys, revealed by a search for sacred geometry and alignments, is the St Michael's Line. First chronicled by John Michell in his book *The View over Atlantis*, the line connects St Michael's Mount in Cornwall to Hopton-on-Sea in Norfolk. Along the way it passes through Glastonbury Tor, Avebury, the abbey at Bury St Edmunds and many ancient churches dedicated to St Michael. The argument goes that this is a *via sacra* – a sacred processional road resembling the one in Ancient Rome that ran up to the Coliseum, passing several temples and monuments – and that segments of it were used as pilgrimage routes. Another line, the Belinus Line, as documented by Gary Biltcliffe and Caroline Hoare in their book *The Spine of Albion*, runs from the Isle of Wight to the tip of northern Scotland, taking in six major cities, including the ancient capitals of England and Scotland.

A search for a ley line by whatever means, and however big or small, can provide motivation for a pilgrimage that takes you to unexpected places and leads you to all kinds of conclusions. For which reason alone, it's worth a go.

Dowsing

Used for generations as a means for finding water, dowsing has more recently been employed for other, more spiritual, activities. Practitioners use one or two metal rods bent into an L-shape, or a pendulum, as a way of tapping into 'earth energies', finding ley lines, and for a variety of other purposes. Dowser Maria Wheatley describes dowsing as 'a good esoteric tool that can tell us what is in our minds, our bodies and our consciousness.' As ancient sites have abundant amounts of what dowsers describe as 'earth energy', they can be a good place to try dowsing. It's important to ask a question first, which can be a simple as 'Is there a ley line running through this monument and, if so, where is it?' When something is found, the rods cross or the pendulum rotates. Some people use dowsing as a method to ask questions about aspects of their life, too. It is an inexact and largely unproven science with a variety of applications, but, in essence, it can be described as a way of revealing non-visible things and getting answers to questions.

Britain's oldest road: the Ridgeway

Many ley lines are said to course through the Neolithic ceremonial landscape at Avebury in Wiltshire. It is unlikely that the locations of the henge, stones and other monuments were randomly chosen. Solar and lunar alignments and, possibly, earth energies may well have played a part, but proximity to a trackway known as the Ridgeway was surely a factor.

This chalk-down ridge, which extends 87 miles from Avebury in Wiltshire to Ivinghoe Beacon on the Chiltern Hills in Hertfordshire, has been walked for at least 5000 years. Rising above the surrounding landscape and dry underfoot, it provided some protection from marauders for drovers moving cattle from the West Country and Wales. It was a safe and relatively level pilgrimage route for anyone heading for one or more of several sites along its length.

As well as Avebury, the Ridgeway connects, bypasses and overlooks many important and probably sacred sites. These include Silbury Hill (see page 65), the Uffington White Horse (see page 138), Wayland's Smithy – a long barrow said to be the burial place of a Neolithic chieftain – and several Iron Age hill forts.

The modern pilgrim would be well advised to walk a section of its route, or take several days to travel its entire length (now a National Trail and clearly waymarked), not just to visit the sacred places along its path but to get a feel for the ancient, relatively unchanged ceremonial landscape all around.

Lych ways: walking the dead home

In the Middle Ages, when people died at home, often in remote communities far from a burial site, the corpse was taken by family and friends – usually in a wagon – along a defined path to a church. In England these paths were called lych ways (they were also known as bier roads or coffin lines) – the word 'lych' is from the Old English for corpse: *liches*. They included a variety of stopping places – a summit of a hill, or near a stream – where the mourners could rest and perform a ritual. In the Lake District, coffin stones can still be found where carried coffins were also laid to give the mourners a rest.

These mournful walks were like sombre pilgrimages, except that one of the party did not return. Although most such routes have vanished, or morphed into footpaths or bridleways, it is still possible to trace them by following clues in the landscape: the name of a field or a church can be a giveaway. Many churches still have their original lychgate – a covered entrance to a churchyard – where the coffin rested before burial. Some lych ways are more obvious: the Lych Way on Dartmoor in Devon – a walk of around 12 miles, depending on which village the procession left from, ending at Lydford Church – is still traceable, and rut marks from the wagons can still be seen.

Similarly, in medieval Holland, the dead were carried for burial along a specially designated straight road called a *dodweg* or death road – laws forbade transporting corpses on other roads. Traces of death roads have also been found in China, Sweden and Costa Rica.

Crossroads: a place of transition

The junction of two paths has rich, often dark, mythological and folkloric associations. Considered a spiritual hinterland, a place that is neither here nor there, a crossroads was a place to contact the otherworld. Supernatural spirits, usually malevolent, could be conjured up here – a demon to broker a deal, perhaps, such as Faust and Mephistopheles in the German legend. They were also associated with the dead – those who could not be buried in Christian burial grounds: suicides, witches, outlaws and gypsies were buried here. On an even grimmer note, until the eighteenth century in England the limbs and torsos of executed criminals were displayed at crossroads as a reminder to others of the consequences of disobedience.

During the Roman invasion, images of the god Hermes (similar to the Celtic god Lugh – Romans and Celts had a lot of gods in common) could sometimes be seen at crossroads. Able to move freely between the worlds of the mortals and the divine, he conducted souls into the afterlife. More cheerfully, he was also able to indicate the right road and to guide travellers' footsteps. Pilgrims and wayfarers would leave an offering to him at the crossroads and hope he would lead them to choose the right path. This is a practice the modern pilgrim might consider reviving!

A mindful pilgrimage along an ancient track

Following a path that has been trodden for centuries connects you to all those people who walked it before. Here are some tips to help you on your way:

- Before you set off, imagine who may have
  followed this route in earlier times. Perhaps
  they were pilgrims walking together to a sacred
  site, or a farmer herding his animals to market,
  or a group of people carrying the dead body
  of a family member to a burial site. The path

exists because many people have walked it, and by walking it yourself, you continue to keep it alive and the way distinct.

- At the start of the walk, pick something off the ground that attracts you. A pebble or a stick that looks like a snake, a shell or an autumnal leaf, say. Put it in your bag and take it with you.

- As you walk, try and view the landscape as your ancestors would have. Do you think it has changed much over the years? Are there new buildings or fewer trees? Perhaps a road now crosses the path or a railway runs alongside it. Or has it remained essentially the same?

- See the landscape as it is now without judgement or speculation. Make simple mental (or written) notes of what you see. Take inspiration from the artist Richard Long, whose art is made by long solitary walks. His series of 'textworks' charts his journey in simple phrases such as 'croaking frogs', 'a large chestnut tree struck down', 'main road', 'buzzards'. He captures the spirit of the place without using loaded language or flowery phrases. Read them and see if you can make similar observations.

- If the path is clearly marked or simple to follow, enjoy the pleasures of walking without a map or GPS. Let the path guide you.

- At the end of the path, leave whatever you picked up at the start on the ground. If the path is short, you could retrace your steps and pick up something new to take back with you and repeat the process.

- Think about when you might return. Walking the same path repeatedly will energise it and you, and you will get to know each other better.

Hamish Fulton – a walking artist

Like Richard Long, the artist Hamish Fulton's work is directly inspired by walking through the landscape. Ancient, well-trodden paths are recurring motifs in his work that focuses on what we overlook as we move along these paths – the ground, the pavement – as well as markers such as boulders and cairns. He has walked a number of pilgrimage routes in the UK, Spain and Japan, and although he thinks walking 'has a life of its own and does not need to be materialised into an artwork', he records what he sees in photographs, illustrations and wall texts. Unlike Richard Long, he makes no interventions in the landscape.

In 1991 he walked all 120 miles of the Pilgrim's Way between Winchester and Canterbury (see page 198) without sleep, and in midwinter. An experience that he said led, unsurprisingly, to hallucinations. More recently, in 2010, he persuaded 200 people to walk seven circuits of Margate's marine bathing pool in silence, keeping a metre's distance from each other. This experience was, like Fulton's solo walks, a meditative experience for all who participated.

2

Water Worlds

*Making a pilgrimage to a well is a mini
adventure, a meeting with a long-lost friend,
a moment of enchantment.*

In the modern age, we take clean water for granted. Turn on
the tap or shower and out it gushes, clear and vital, keeping
us clean and hydrated. It's only when there is a drought or a
water shortage that we realise how essential it really is. For our
ancestors, whose survival depended on having a reliable, local
source, discovering a spring of bubbling, crystal-clear water
must have felt like a miracle or a gift from the gods. No surprise, then, that the spring has been considered sacred by most
of the world's religions, which have worshipped and attributed
to it all manner of supernatural powers – from healing to
fertility-boosting and predicting the future.

Many myths and legends have sprung up around watery places. Water has seemingly magical powers: it moves like a living creature and it shape shifts – at times it is a quiet trickle or a still pool, and at others a furious cacophony of foam and spray. It is both life-giving and destructive; still and tranquil; ferocious and deafening. In Norse and Celtic mythology, wells were regarded as portals to the Otherworld. The water, bubbling or gushing from an unseen source beneath the earth, could only be explained as a gift from a supernatural being. Springs, rivers, ponds and lakes were all said to have the souls of spirits, which had to be nurtured with offerings and rituals.

My favourite wells are the forgotten ones. The wells that trickle from a wall beside a busy road and are ignored by passers-by, or that are submerged beneath undergrowth beside a hedge at the edge of a field – those that have consistently issued water for centuries, whether anyone cared if they did or not. Making a pilgrimage to find a neglected well, after reading about it in a local history book or discovering a W symbol on an OS map and then venturing out and finding it, is a mini adventure, a meeting with a long-lost friend, a moment of enchantment. Dipping a hand into its cool, clear water then splashing it on your face is an awakening, a re-energising of the well and of yourself.

I have visited the island of Iona in the Scottish Hebrides many times since childhood, but it is never enough. It's one of those places that constantly draws me back with its unique, charged atmosphere and its dreamlike landscape of stone cottages, Abbey, turquoise sea and white sand. Although it is tiny (2km long and 6km wide), it packs a big spiritual punch and has always been a place of pilgrimage. It played a major part in the formation of the early Christian Church thanks to the arrival from Ireland of St Columba, who founded a monastery there in AD 563, and it continues to attract pilgrims of various faiths and beliefs. Some come to go on retreat, some come for the day on the ferry from Mull just to look around, and others, like me, come simply to spend time in its peaceful surroundings.

During one visit I stayed with the Findhorn Foundation, a spiritual community. They have a house on the island called Traigh Bhan, which they open for quiet contemplation, meditation and spiritual retreats. One of the team members that ran it told me that close to the island's highest point, Dun I (which is not very high: just 101m above sea level) was the Well of Eternal Youth (Tobar nah Aois). Pilgrims, she told me, had been known to bathe there at dawn to restore their youthful powers.

Intrigued by the fairy-tale-sounding name, and hoping for some regenerating magic to turn back time, I set off to find it the next morning. (But not at dawn, I'm afraid to say – the bed was too comfortable.) The walk didn't take long – nothing is very far away on Iona – but the sun was out and the sea sparkled, so I took my time and walked slowly, stopping every so often to look around and drink up the scene. I always savour every moment on the island, knowing that soon I will be back experiencing everyday life with all its mundane, and often irritating, concerns.

I had read on the island's website that Tobar nah Aois is associated with the Irish sixth-century Saint Brigid, a favourite saint of mine (more about her later), who was supposed to have visited Iona at midnight one summer solstice. The word

'Hebrides' means 'The Islands of Bride (Brigid)' so her presence is felt all over the region. It wasn't midnight or the summer solstice on my visit – just a regular day in May – but the path to the well, through bog and over tufty grass and rocky outcrops, felt suitably enchanted.

On arrival at Dun I, I stopped to savour the wrap-around views of the island and the sea surrounding it before looking for the Well. Despite its size, there is an amazing sense of openness and breadth on Iona. You feel like you can really breathe. It took a few minutes of poking around in heather and looking over boulders to find the well, which made me appreciate it more when I did.

What I discovered was a small, freshwater pool bordered by rock on one side and moorland on the other and which, on that Spring morning, reflected the blue sky and the clouds above. I knelt beside it and dipped my hands in its chilly water. Legend has it that if you wash your face in the well on May Day morning, you will stay eternally young. I'd missed the actual moment by a few days, but I gave it a go anyway. I splashed the water on my face – a startling moment that brought me fully into the present – then rubbed my skin dry with the sleeve of my jumper. It was probably the coldness of the water that did it, but my eyes felt wide and open, as though I could see more clearly and for a greater distance. I had woken up.

The spiritual power of water

The healing and purifying power of water has always been recognised by major religions and faiths. Christians dip their fingers into the water of a special basin (sacrarium) as they enter a church and then make the sign of the cross. They also baptise their children in a font. Aboriginal people in Australia, recognising that water is essential for survival, make it part of their culture – water is represented by the Rainbow Serpent, the giver of life. When a rainbow is seen in the sky, it is supposed to be the Rainbow Serpent travelling from one waterhole to another. The Hindu practice of total immersion in the sacred River Ganges during the Kumbh Mela festival (see page 210) is believed to wash away sins and free bathers from the cycle of death and rebirth.

Holy, healing wells

Our Celtic ancestors would only visit sacred wells at certain, more potent times of year. May Day and Midsummer were most often chosen, being the two turning points of the calendar when the gates of the Otherworld were said to open, and when the veil between it and the temporal world was thinnest. This was the time to communicate with the dead, seek wisdom from spirits (pixies and fairies were rumoured to make an appearance) and ask for healing – and a sacred well or a spring was the place to do it.

Water from holy wells has been used in rituals to heal conditions ranging from warts to broken bones, rheumatism and poor vision. This is a practice that continues on a major scale at wells where holy visions are said to have taken place, such as the pilgrimage site of Lourdes in France (see page 44). It's a tradition to leave an offering at a well, either in gratitude for a prayer answered, to ask for help, or to safeguard the future. This is why better-known wells are often adorned with strips of cloth (known as clootie rags: from the Old English *clut*, meaning 'a piece of cloth'), piles of stones and other bits and pieces, and why bent silver pins are sometimes thrown in (a practice that morphed into dropping coins into fountains to bring good luck).

A refreshing pilgrimage

In Europe, pilgrimage to holy wells was at its height in the Middle Ages. Originally places of Celtic worship, they became adopted by the Church, which Christianised them by naming them after its saints, or by building a church near, or on top of, a well. Some wells had stone structures built around them to keep the water clean and to provide places for pilgrims to sit, bathe and even sleep. Although many of these buildings are now in ruins, the water continues to flow and is there waiting to be discovered.

The mysterious, lucid and mutable nature of water has meant that it is also associated with intuition and the subconscious. Some wells, like Madron Well in Cornwall, are said to be 'dream temples' where the pilgrim would sleep on a stone seat near the water, preferably at midsummer, hoping to dream a healing dream or to foretell the future.

Nowadays, making a pilgrimage to a place of water gives us a chance to think about it in all its wonderful manifestations. This could be a walk to a sacred well or a healing spring, a trip to the banks of a river (or one following it from its source to sea, see below), a hike up a hill to find a waterfall (also reputed to have healing properties), or a search for a secret lake to swim in.

Wanting to be near water is a fundamental impulse in all of us, even if it's a simple desire to pile into the car and head for the sea on a hot summer's day. Better, though, to pick your destination carefully and set off steadily on foot, anticipating the enchanting and refreshing journey's end as you walk towards it.

From the source to the sea: river journeys

The linear course of a river makes it a natural route for a pilgrimage. Rising unassumingly as a small stream, the water course quickly gathers momentum, speed and volume as other streams, rainwater, underground springs and other sources join it on its way towards the sea. Often it is hard to pinpoint exactly where a river starts. It could begin its journey in a lake with other rivers or it could begin life as one of several tributaries. Some of the world's major rivers, such as the Nile, have several possible sources.

Similarly, the exact position of the headwaters of the River Thames is disputed. Thames Head near the village of Kemble in Gloucestershire is marked with an ancient ash tree and a plaque but often there is no sign of water, although on damper days a spring can be seen emerging from the hillside and forming a pool at the foot of the stone. Nearby, Trewsbury Mead, near Cirencester, is the Environment Agency's candidate for the Thames headwater and the site is marked on OS maps, but similarly it is visible only during rainy spells. It is also the start of the Thames Path public footpath: a 194-km walk that will take you to the sea.

Walking the length of a river is a romantic and appealing notion and provides a clear path for a pilgrimage. Two examples of the life-changing nature of such journeys have been chronicled by the authors Olivia Laing and Katharine Norbury. In *To the River* Olivia Laing writes about her 42-mile walk along the River Ouse from Haywards Heath, over the South Downs, to the English Channel at Newhaven. In *The Fish Ladder* Katharine Norbury reverses the journey and follows various rivers from the sea to their source, sometimes accompanied by her daughter Evie, as a way to try and deal with a series of personal tragedies. Both books are inspirational to those wanting to make a similar pilgrimage of their own.

Wild swimming pilgrimages

Anyone who has swum outdoors knows its particular pleasures: the shock of plunging into cold water, followed by the refreshing all-over body tingle; the delight of swimming with a duck at eye level; the wonder of floating on your back and watching clouds scud overhead; the satisfyingly warm rub with a rough towel afterwards. It is an experience far removed from overheated, and often overcrowded, public pools. Another benefit is that, like walking, outdoor swimming is absolutely free and anyone can do it at any time that suits them. Combine walking and swimming by heading to a well, lake, river or stretch of coastline that has meaning to you and where you can swim, and you'll have a pilgrimage well worth making.

Although places to swim outdoors are limited and must be chosen wisely, there is plenty of advice on where to go. The Outdoor Swimming Society and the River and Lake Swimming Association have lists of recommended places and offer tips on what to wear and how to behave. There are also several excellent books about outdoor swimming, Kate Rew's *Wild Swim* and Daniel Start's *Wild Swimming* being two of the first and best.

Pilgrimages to sacred wells and springs

A natural spring is a modest thing, bubbling quietly from the ground or gently welling from a rock. This belies its importance, both practically in terms of life-giving sustenance, and as a place of spiritual meaning. Similarly, from the surface, depending on the structure that surrounds it, a well can easily be overlooked, but this disguises its depths – literally and spiritually.

As the power and potency of certain wells and springs were recognised, they grew in stature and prestige. Although not all of them are as venerated as much today, they are still powerful and peaceful places to visit. The following are all recognised pilgrimage destinations for different faiths and beliefs.

Chalice Well, Glastonbury, Somerset, England

Situated at the base of Glastonbury Tor, a distinctive hill overlooking the Isle of Avalon, Glastonbury and Somerset, the Chalice Well is one of the most famous in the world and is steeped in mystery and legend. A natural spring fed by an aquifer, it has been in use for around two thousand years, unfailingly delivering water at the rate of 1,100,000 litres per day at a steady temperature of 11°C.

This constancy, and the water's reddish hue (from its iron oxide content), make the spring special, but when these elements are combined with Christian and Arthurian myths, they gain even greater potency. Christian legend has it that after the crucifixion of Jesus, Joseph of Arimathea, a secret disciple, came to Glastonbury with the Holy Grail (the chalice that Christ used at the Last Supper and which caught drops of blood at his crucifixion). He placed the chalice under the well, and it supposedly turned the water blood-red. The chalice was later sought by King Arthur's knights as a sacred quest and is central to the Arthurian legends concerning the Isle of Avalon (so named because the Tor was once surrounded by sea).

Glastonbury Tor and the Chalice Well were places of pilgrimage and ritual prior to the Christian presence and they continue to be important sites for believers of all faiths today. While some believe that the blood-red chalybeate (mineral-rich) water represents the blood of Christ, others see it as symbolising the menstrual blood of the Goddess and its abundance, earth's fertility.

Wander around the well The lid of the well is decorated with two overlapping circles. This is a *vesica piscis* (literally, 'the bladder of a fish' – it resembles the conjoined dual air bladders of fish), an example of ancient and sacred geometry. Wander in the gardens and find the ancient yew trees. There are plenty of places to sit quietly and soak up the atmosphere. The Chalice Well Trust looks after the well and holds music and poetry events in the gardens, designed to complement meditation and contemplation at the well.

Mount Shasta springs, Siskiyou County, California, USA

Mount Shasta, a dormant volcano that towers 4300m over its surroundings, is one of the seven sacred mountains of the world. It has long been revered by the Native American people, who equally value the rivers, lakes and springs that surround it. For indigenous people, water not only sustains life, it is sacred. Springs, rivers and waterfalls were thought to be created by the Great Spirit and seen as places of healing and magic, inhabited by divine beings and animals. To drink and bathe in the mountain's waters connects with this magical realm, lengthens life and boosts good health.

Tales of the medicinal properties of the Mount Shasta springs, which had been used by indigenous people for thousands of years, led to many of the springs being seized by people with profit in mind. In the late nineteenth and early twentieth centuries, the Shasta Springs resort opened above the Mossbrae Falls, bringing tourists in great numbers to sample the healing power of the water. The resort closed in the 1950s, but the springs and lake continue to draw visitors.

Start at the source You could start your journey in the City Park. Here you will find the Big Springs headwaters, the source of the Sacramento River, which gushes out of a small grotto into a shallow pool before cascading through the valley. Like many springs, its water, which comes from an aquifer and has filtered through volcanic rock, is said to have health benefits. Local people collect the water to drink and to cook with, despite signs warning against it. Take a small bottle along and run the water through a filter before sampling some yourself, or wash your hands and face in the constant, refreshing stream. Alternatively, head for Panther Meadows, 22km east of the city of Mount Shasta, and halfway up the mountain. A trail to its northern end will take you through the Meadows to a small spring flowing from a rocky outcrop, regarded as sacred by indigenous tribes.

Sanctuary of Our Lady of Lourdes, France

Although now a major destination for Roman Catholic pilgrims, it has been suggested that the grotto at Lourdes was once a place of pagan veneration. This seems likely as many ancient sacred spaces were adopted by Christianity, with springs being especially susceptible.

The small town in the Hautes-Pyrénées region of southwestern France found itself at the centre of religious fervour in 1858 when, on 11 February, a fourteen-year-old girl called Bernadette Soubirous claimed to have seen the Virgin Mary eighteen times. The vision took place at the Massabielle grotto under a rocky outcrop near the River Gave de Pau. The Virgin directed Bernadette to scratch at the earth with a stick and drink from the spring that bubbled up. When word got out, sick people visited the spring and 'miracles' ensued.

Despite the Church's initial caution and request for evidence, news of the miracles quickly spread and soon Lourdes became a place of mass pilgrimage. Nowadays, six million people visit each year and there have been sixty-nine verified miracles or cures. Water now flows freely from the source of the spring – enough for pilgrims to bathe in. Not everyone comes to be cured, however (the water has been tested and has no curative properties). Many visit the grotto to pray to the Virgin Mary, as an act of penance, or in gratitude for a prayer fulfilled.

Broaden your pilgrimage Don't confine yourself to the grotto, and don't be limited by your belief. It is a place for everyone to come and reflect, set intentions or offer a prayer. There are various pilgrimage options on the official website, including one-day and fifteen-day pilgrimages. The relatively new 'Project Grotto, the Heart of Lourdes', takes pilgrims on a journey around the town, starting with a visit to the grotto and ending with the lighting of a candle on the other side of the river.

Madron Well, West Penwith, Cornwall, England

Although there are around a hundred sacred wells in Cornwall, Madron Well outside Penzance is the best known and most visited. The approach to the well – a 15-minute walk along a pathway lined with twisted hawthorn trees and abundant ferns – sets a magical atmosphere. On arrival, you will find a small, ruined, roofless chapel built in Christian times, and a tree festooned with clootie rags above a wishing well. Nearby, hidden in undergrowth, is the actual well: a granite opening in the ground bubbling with spring water.

The well is named after St Madron (also known as St Mardren), about whom very little is known, except that he or she is rumoured to have died c.545 (some say on 20 June, the summer solstice) and may have been responsible for various miracles.

The well's reputed magical and healing powers have made it a pilgrimage site for centuries – it was a Cornish Celtic sacred site long before the chapel was built – with the sick and suffering coming to dip themselves in its water, often on May Day, hoping for a cure. The tying of a clootie rag to a tree or bush nearby was a supplementary boost. Scraps of cloth tied to a branch were accompanied by a wish or prayer, and, as the piece of cloth deteriorated, the supplicant's condition would, hopefully, improve. Young women also came to the well to see how long they would have to wait to get married. As they asked the question, they threw two pieces of straw fastened with a pin into the water: the ensuing bubbles were carefully counted – each one represented a year to go.

The well is still visited by the sick, needy and hopeful – the evidence is dangling from the tree adorned with clootie rags and all manner of other offerings, including toys and poems. It is also a peaceful and calm place simply to visit, sit beside and be still.

Go with an intention This is a perfect opportunity to address something that may be troubling you, or to ask for help or healing. Cut a strip of biodegradable material (such as cotton or some other natural fibre) and tie it carefully to the clootie tree as you bring your intention to mind. Alternatively, you could drop a bent silver pin into the well and focus your thoughts around that.

Saint Brigid's Well, Liscannor, County Clare, Ireland

In Ireland, pilgrimage to holy wells are still an important part of the Christian year. Ireland has more wells in active use than any other country, and the country's Celtic past is still very much in evidence. Many pilgrimages take place on the Celtic festival of Imbolc (1st and 2nd February), which not only marks the beginning of spring but is also St Brigid's Day. St Brigid – also known as Bridgit, Bride and Brighid – is the second most popular saint in Ireland (St Patrick tops the chart) and many wells are dedicated to her. Formerly a Celtic goddess, she was said to have been born at dawn's first light wearing a crown of fire and is a deity of fire as well as fertility (both human and animal), craft and poetry. The seventh-century saint Broccan described her as an 'excellent woman, a flame, golden, delightful. May she, the sun-dazzling, splendid, guide us to the eternal Kingdom.'

St Brigid's Well at Liscannor is one of many wells scattered over Ireland that is dedicated to her (there are also several in Scotland) and it is regarded as having healing powers. Tucked into a stone grotto, it is a popular destination for Christian and secular pilgrims who come here to petition for the sick or to give thanks. The well is surrounded by mementoes, including rosaries, written prayers, requests, and votive candles. Legend has it that Brigid plucked out her eyes out and threw them at a suitor but regained sight when she washed out the sockets at one of her wells. Consequently, many people with eyesight problems come to the well to ask Brigid to restore their vision.

Avoid the rush Try and get there early in the morning or late in the day to avoid the crowds. You don't need to be sick or in need to visit the well – it's worth visiting for its atmosphere alone. It's also a good place to get to know St Brigid better: she is a saint/goddess of intriguing complexity and influence.

Saint Winefride's Well, Holywell, Flintshire, Wales

This ancient well has been a place of pilgrimage since the twelfth century, with pilgrims drawn by the promise of its miraculous healing powers. Unlike many other pilgrimage destinations, it was spared destruction during the Reformation, making it one of the oldest pilgrimage sites in the UK. It is also the start of the pilgrimage route to Bardsey Island (see page 214), which runs the length of the Llyn Peninsula.

Legend has it that the spring rose from the ground in AD 660 at the spot where the head of St Winefride (Gwenfrewi) fell after it was severed by a local prince, Caradoc. He had made unwelcome advances, which Winefride rejected. Her uncle, St Beuno, found the head and placed it back on her body, prayed, and brought her back to life. Winefride spent the rest of her life as a nun.

The well is housed in a fine sixteenth-century building and chapel. It has an outdoor pool where the faithful still come to be cured.

Take the plunge Go for full immersion in the outdoor pool, which is fed by the well. There are poolside tents available to slip into your costume, and the water is shallow enough to sit in until you are too cold to sit any longer.

The intricate art of well dressing

Our forefathers regarded wells and springs as mysterious and unknowable. Bursting or bubbling from the ground, the water they provided was a basic necessity of life, without which man and beast would perish. As such, they were regarded with awe and considered the dwelling places of powerful spirits – the only explanation for the continual existence of such a vital element of daily life. Veneration of wells was important to maintain a lively flow of water, and they were honoured with rituals, dances and flower decoration.

With the arrival of Christianity to Britain, water worship was forbidden. Instead, wells were rededicated to the Virgin Mary or a saint. The dressing of wells with flowers continued, however, but now as a thanksgiving to God rather than to placate water spirits.

It's a tradition that is still practised in the Peak District, Derbyshire on the well's saint's day, when wells are adorned with intricate scenes. Some, but not all, are taken from the Bible and are fashioned from overlapping flower heads, leaves and berries. Wells are dressed by a team of people ▶

who insert living plants into panels of wet clay, a process that can take days to complete. Most wells are then blessed in a ceremony, which is followed by a carnival or festival in the village.

Notable well dressing festivals include Tissington, a village in Derbyshire, which has five wells – Holy Well, Coffin Well, Hand's Well, the Town Well and Yew Tree Well – all of which are elaborately dressed to celebrate Ascension Day every year. The town of Buxton decorates two wells every July – a good reason to hold an annual festival with its own Wells Festival Queen.

A mindful journey to a well

Many wells have been abandoned and neglected and can be hard to find; often they are hidden by undergrowth or tucked away in the corner of a field. Seeking them out, wherever they may be, is part of the pilgrimage. Local guidebooks and histories are a good place to start, or you can scour an OS map and look for clues (the symbol for a well is a blue W, and the symbol for a spring is a blue SPR). Some wells are still a place of pilgrimage and clearly signposted, and those by churches are usually cared for and easy to locate. Whatever type of well you are looking for, approach it the same way: with reverence and care.

As you near the well, slow your pace and pay attention to what surrounds you. Wells are often found at the end of shady rural lanes – notice how the light filters through the branches, creating patterns from the shadows. If it is a wet day, let the rain fall softly on your head and shoulders, and accept it rather than resist it. The Earth needs the rain as much as it needs the sun. Stop every so often and remind yourself why you are making this pilgrimage. Do you have an intention in mind? If you do, this is the time to repeat it to yourself.

If you are walking across a field and can see the well in the distance, step steadily towards your goal and notice as it grows larger in your field of vision. If you are heading towards a well in a city or town, be aware of other people and traffic but don't let them bother you – keep moving onwards with your destination in mind.

And when you get there ... As you get your first glimpse of the well, stop for a moment or two before making the final steps. Consider your journey to the well and what it has meant so far. Acknowledge the well, then approach it. When you arrive beside it, you might like to:

- **Hang a rag on a nearby tree.** Branches of wells that are still visited by pilgrims are often festooned with clootie rags left as votive offerings, perhaps to ask for a cure or as the representation of a prayer. If you choose to add one yourself, make sure the material you use is biodegradable. Not only is this environmentally friendly, it is said that as the cloth deteriorates the ailment disappears, or the prayer is answered. Dunk the rag in the well first, then tie it to a branch with the others. Alternatively, you could leave something natural like a flower, a pine cone, a stone or a crystal. Don't be tempted to move or remove any offerings that are already there: superstition has it that any illness asked to be cured by whoever left it, will be transferred to the taker.

- **Leave some silver.** Traditionally, bent pins are dropped into a well as an offering. You could do the same but be wary of cluttering up this special place.
- **Take a dip.** If the well or spring is big enough, and you have a towel or change of clothes, get right in and immerse yourself. The water is inviting you to refresh your mind and your body, and dunking yourself in it is the best way to do this. If your destination is a river, lake or the edge of an ocean, now could be the time for a spot of wild swimming. At least put your hands in and splash your face and neck. Some spiritual practitioners also recommend dabbing your third eye (between the eyes) with spring water.
- **Drink the water**. But only if you have filtered it first. If you don't have a filter, fill a small bottle and take it with you on your return journey. When you come to another well, empty the contents – this will create a spiritual connection between the two wells.
- **Sit beside it for a while.** After your walk, you will need a moment or two to recharge and

refresh, and now you have reached this unique place it would be a shame to rush away. Some pools and springs feel fathomless and eternal and are a good place to meditate. They may also boost your creativity and inspire you to sketch, to paint or to write a poem. Remember to take a notebook with you to capture any thoughts.

3

The Mighty Mountain

Climb a mountain and you find yourself where
the sun rises sooner and sets later, where the air
is clearer, the light is brighter, and where
ordinary life feels very far away.

Every April I go walking with three friends, usually somewhere in the UK. Over the years, we have tramped along
coastal paths, over downs and across moors. It rains quite
heavily for much of the time. One year we decided that, for
a change, we didn't want to get soaked, so we headed to the
Alicante mountains in Spain. And, sure enough, we avoided
the rain. Instead we got plenty of sun and plenty of mountains.

It was my first experience of scaling mountains of a significant height. Ones that make you puff and pant and stop
frequently to 'admire the view'. Arrival at each summit

provoked feelings of exhaustion and exhilaration. From a breezy rocky outcrop on top of one, we could see the hotels of Benidorm in the distance, lining the coast. Not far away but a very different world. Climbing mountains does this: in a short time, you find yourself in an alternative universe – a universe where the temperature and the weather is different, where the sun rises sooner and sets later, where the air is clearer (and sometimes thinner), the light is brighter, and where ordinary life feels very far away.

As we sat slackjawed at the view, a lone walker approached. He had the look of a beat poet or a ragged philosopher about him. He told us that he had been living in the mountains for six months, climbing one peak after another, sleeping out, drinking from springs. It was like a religious experience, he said, and the thought of descending back into 'normal' life was one he kept postponing, although it was, of course, inevitable.

I thought of him a couple of years later as I set off on a solo mini pilgrimage across Cornwall. Unlike him, though, I had a clear route and destination: along the St Michael's Way, a 19.5-km pilgrimage from Lelant on the north coast to St Michael's Mount on the south. Also, unlike him, I was only away from home for a couple of nights. But I was heading for a holy mountain and hoping for some sort of transformative experience along the way, or at least some time to clear my head.

St Michael's Way is clearly waymarked with scallop shells (the pilgrim's symbol and icon of St James), and pilgrims can pick up a passport to be stamped at certain places on the route. It's thought that the Way was once part of a greater network of pilgrimage routes that lead to St James' Cathedral in Santiago de Compostela in northern Spain. Rather than sail the dangerous seas around Land's End, Irish and Welsh pilgrims took the safer pedestrian route across the Cornish peninsula. The scallop shells and passport are a reminder of this, and walking the Way now counts towards Santiago's Pilgrim Certificate and makes for a pleasing connection with the Camino.

From the peaceful church of St Uny at Lelant, the route coursed along the coastal path, past a holy well, then headed inland towards Trencrom Hill. It was a short and not particularly difficult ascent to the top, but it was roasting hot and took me a little longer than it would normally. Besides, I was in no hurry. The path wound around the hill and through a couple of upright stones, which felt like a gateway, to the top.

Trencrom Hill is a fine example of a 'mountjoy' – a hill where pilgrims see the destination for the first time – and I could clearly spot St Michael's Mount topped by its castle way ahead. Surrounded by the glittering sea, it looked mythical and romantic. The Mount is a tidal island – like that other pilgrim favourite, the holy island of Lindisfarne in Northumberland – so is only accessible by foot at low tide. Being neither totally in the sea or part of the land is what makes these places especially holy, it is said. St Michael's Mount would make a fitting end to my mini pilgrimage.

Trencrom Hill is the site of a Neolithic fort and there is evidence of former habitation – stones in positions that could have once been occupied by walls, a rock basin, a well – scattered about between rocks and boulders. The fort certainly has a good vantage point: the entire coastline of the Land's End peninsula, including Mount's Bay and the Hayle Estuary, was visible from up there, laid out before me, looking splendid.

I found a sheltered spot in a sun-warmed cairn and opened my Thermos. A cup of tea later and my eyes started to close. Falling asleep on top of the hill, just for a few minutes, was a delicious treat and hard to resist. A couple of children ran past and startled me awake, but after a moment or two of disorientation I was back on my feet.

Further on down the hill, I stopped for the night at a B&B, so that the following morning I could complete my pilgrimage refreshed. The next day it was both liberating and uplifting to set off early on my own with just a rucksack and a purpose. As I walked tree-lined lanes, trudged over fields, and finally strode along a great sweep of beach, the world opened up and small but unexpected things happened. I met a lost dog and restored him to his owner. A friendly woman let me into Tremenheere Sculpture Gardens (worth a pilgrimage itself) early so I had it to myself. Passersby said hello and waved cheerily.

By the time I got to Marazion, the small town near the Mount, my mood was buoyant. I entered All Saints Church in the town to get my passport stamped, spent some time reading the information about St Michael's Way posted on its walls and then sat quietly for a moment. It was at this point I was surprised to find myself in tears. I've still no idea why. I hadn't come very far and it hadn't been particularly difficult, but it did feel significant for a reason I couldn't name. I lit a candle and thought of family members and friends who had died – something it always feels right to do in churches – and then left the peaceful place and walked the final leg.

It was high summer, so crossing the causeway to the Mount meant that there were plenty of visitors taking selfies, jostling one another and eating ice cream. Together we made a shambling and scattered procession to the castle, then up the steps to the chapel. The way to the top is, fittingly, along the Pilgrim's Way, a path uncovered in the 1950s and one that was much used by pilgrims in the Middle Ages. It was steep enough to remind me that I was on a pilgrimage and not on a day trip. At the top there was the castle to explore and, finally, the heart-stopping view of coastline, ocean and sky: big, bright and beautiful. A view, I thought, that the ragged Spanish philosopher would also have loved. The combination of effort, purpose and reward is what a mountain pilgrimage is all about after all.

On top of the world

Of all pilgrimages, one to the top of a mountain is the most dramatic. Unlike a level walk, an ascent has the additional elements of danger and unpredictability. Up there the weather has a habit of changing in a minute: sunshine can be chased away by pelting rain or smothered by mist; the terrain alters as you rise, from grassy foothills to barren rock; the seasons shift – it may be summer below but, as you ascend, it is suddenly spring. When the summit is reached, however, and all this has been overcome, there is a sense of having done something significant, of having actually arrived, safe and sound. The journey can also have a profound spiritual meaning.

High places have been a place of pilgrimage for many cultures since ancient times, their altitude considered a means of getting closer to the gods, physically and metaphysically.

Soaring into the sky while remaining rooted in the earth, mountains are a link between heaven and earth. Venerated accordingly, they are thresholds between this world and the next, are considered the homes of the gods and consequently bestowed with holiness.

In Ancient Greek mythology, Mount Olympus – the highest mountain in the country – was where the gods lived. The Peruvian Incas living in the Andes made child sacrifices to the gods on their highest peaks and thought their mountain villages were gateways to the land of their gods. Jesus preached the Beatitudes, part of his Sermon on the Mount, on a mountain near the Sea of Galilee in Israel. The Japanese religion Shugendō puts climbing mountains at the centre of its practice. (Before the sixth century, the Japanese thought mountains too holy for humans and worshipped respectfully from a distance.) The Navajo and Hopi Indians also considered mountains sacred. Navajo Mountain in Arizona still holds an important place in their traditions – their name for it is 'Heart of the Earth' – and continues to be a place of pilgrimage. And in Germany and Scandinavia, the gods Wotan and Odin each had their own mountains.

Considering their size, unreachability and presence, it's unsurprising that mountains have always had a spiritual significance for religions worldwide. The summit – that unknown place far from daily life – being particularly bewitching. Rising to a dizzying place above the clouds, often covered with snow and glaciers – mountains are the 'White Lands' of the gods, where spirits might ascend to heaven, and where man might come closer to the Otherworld.

Mountains also, of course, draw mountaineers intent on immersing themselves in the difficult challenges they present.

The Tuscan scholar Petrach, who climbed Mount Ventoux in Provence in 1335, claimed to have been the first man to climb a mountain for its own sake and to enjoy the view, but many others followed and continue to do so.

Tibetan Buddhists, on the other hand, would not dream of climbing to the top of a mountain (see Mount Kailash, below). To set foot on its slopes is seen as a sin. Instead, they walk respectfully around its base. As Nan Shepherd writes in her book *The Living Mountain*, which chronicles her walks on her beloved Cairngorms in Scotland, there is much to be said for walking around, over and across a mountain rather than charging up it, intent solely on reaching the summit.

How you approach a mountain for your personal pilgrimage is up to you. Heading for the hills, whatever the reason, is always a good idea: they rarely disappoint.

Cairns: wayside reminders

As you climb a mountain path, chances are that every so often you will come across piles of stones heaped into rough pyramids. These cairns have been created by travellers and pilgrims, who each left a stone as they walked past. They reassure walkers that they are on the right track and are reminders of those who have passed that way before them – each stone represents one person. They are a way of keeping to the path and connecting with fellow pilgrims from the past and the future. ▶

A word of caution: these days many quiet and remote spots are cluttered with stacked stones in teetering piles. These have no purpose as waymarks and hold no spiritual meaning. Instead, they have mostly been constructed for social media opportunities and are an irritating addition to the landscape. Be mindful about the stones you leave and where you leave them.

Pilgrimages to mountains and hills

Despite their constant, steady and towering presence, mountains are often ignored and relegated to a mere backdrop to daily life. It is easy to resist their calling, take them for granted and never set foot on their slopes. If there is one, or a range of mountains, near you that you are still to explore, now is the time to do it. If there isn't one nearby, think about making a pilgrimage to a mountain you feel a connection with. You will be following in the footsteps of pilgrims of all beliefs, who have walked their varied slopes – from the cone of the volcanic Mount Fuji in Japan to the vast sandstone plug that is Uluru in Australia.

Mount Fuji, Japan

Still classified as an active volcano (although its last eruption was in 1707), the distinctive cone shape and height (3766m) of Mount Fuji makes it one of the world's most recognisable mountains. Considered sacred by several faiths, including Buddhism, Shinto and Shugendō (Shugendō followers are called *yamabushi*, which means 'mountain priests'), it has been a popular pilgrimage destination since the fifteenth century. Myths abound about its divine origins, spiritual powers and resident gods, and it is surrounded by temples and shrines of various religions, which have even been built right at the edge of the crater.

The highest and most prominent peak in Japan, Mount Fuji has become a national symbol and is represented in art throughout history, most notably in Katsushika Houkusai's woodblock prints *Thirty-six Views of Mount Fuji*.

Although still a popular pilgrimage site, tourists now outnumber pilgrims on the mountain's slopes. The walk to the top is hard work and not especially scenic – the terrain is barren and rocky – but the view from the summit rewards the endeavour.

Get there for sunrise Allow between four and eight hours to reach the summit, depending on your sprightliness. The official climbing season runs from 1 July to 26 August, when the mountain is usually snow-free and the weather is mild. Climbing to the top is a popular activity (around 300,000 people do so every year), so be prepared for company – queues can form in places, although weekdays are a little quieter. Most climbers aim to arrive at the top for sunrise, so either stretch the climb over two days, staying overnight in a mountain hut, or walk through the night by torchlight.

Mount Kailash, Tibet

No one has ever climbed to the summit of Mount Kailash, but every year thousands of pilgrims make the great trek to see it. It is the object of one of the most devout and flourishing pilgrimages in the world. Rather than scramble to its snow-capped top like other sacred mountains, pilgrims walk reverently around its base. This circumambulation is known as *kora* in Tibetan and is a tradition that extends back thousands of years. Circling a sacred place or thing is a ritual common to many of the world's religions: in Islam, pilgrims on the Hajj walk around the holy Kaaba seven times. The Tibetan word for pilgrimage is *neykhor*, which means to circle around a holy place. The goal is not to reach a particular destination but to transcend ignorance and materialism, reaching enlightenment by walking. Sacred sites, like Mount Kailash, are called *neys* to remind Buddhist pilgrims of this.

Mount Kailash is a four-sided mass of black rock with a river originating from each side. Capped with a dome of ice, it rises magnificently from an immense plateau. It's easy to see why it is one of the most venerated places in the world – it is spectacular.

Kailash is considered sacred in four religions: Hinduism, Buddhism, Bon (the indigenous religion of Tibet pre-Buddhism) and Jainism. Hindus believe that it is the home of Shiva, the hedonistic four-armed mountain god, and is where he brought the goddess Parvati to live with him. Buddhists consider it to be the navel of the world, its absolute centre. All four faiths have it at the heart of their beliefs and all believe that, while a pilgrimage there is a necessary spiritual act, to set foot on its higher slopes is a sin.

Easier to reach now than in the past – the drive from Lhasa takes four hours and helicopters are even known to fly there – it still takes a lot of determination to reach Mount Kailash, which, of course, is all part of the pilgrimage. The walk around the mountain takes about three days at a reasonable pace (luggage is carried by yak) although some especially speedy pilgrims do it in a day, and others, prostrating themselves over and over, take weeks. Along the path are monasteries, hermit caves and hundreds of little cairns left by previous pilgrims, each inscribed with the sacred Tibetan mantra *Om Mani Padme Hum*.

For a first-hand account of a pilgrimage to Mount Kailash, read *To a Mountain in Tibet* by Colin Thubron.

Prepare to be seriously challenged The *kora* is 52km long, and it starts loftily at 4600m above sea level, rising to 5600m at the pass. Also, choose your dates carefully: Tibet is closed for most of February and March, and you will need a permit to travel. May, June, late August and September are the best times.

Silbury Hill, Avebury, Wiltshire, England

The shape of Silbury Hill gives it away. No natural hill looks like this: conical with steep, even sides and a level, flat top. It rises from the surrounding fields as if it's been turned out from a pudding basin. It is, in fact, the largest man-made prehistoric mound in Europe (it's 30m high) and was constructed from half a million tonnes of material – mostly chalk – a process that probably took several generations of toil to accomplish.

It is obviously a mound of some significance, but the reason for its construction still puzzles archaeologists. Repeated excavations (the last one from 1968 to 1969) quashed the notion that it was a burial mound. No grave goods or bones were found. What was discovered, however, was its sophisticated structure: a primary mound was built from blocks of chalk, filled in between with rubble, and this took the form of a seven-sided pyramid. Earth was then piled on top and the structure was grassed over, creating the shape it has retained for over 4500 years.

The other revealing discovery was vegetation that was radio-carbon dated to a notable time during 2660 BC: between the last week of July and the first week of August. At the midway point is 2 August, the time of Lughnasadh – the harvest festival later called Lammas. This has led to speculation that the hill was created to celebrate the harvest, a similar idea to Scottish Lammas towers, which were constructed in Scotland up until the eighteenth century. What is certain is that it was (and still is) a special place where people assembled, most likely for a spiritual purpose. The henge at Avebury and its stone circle was also built around this time, so, in all likelihood, Silbury Hill was one element of a larger sacred complex that stretched across Wiltshire.

Also visit nearby sites Don't forget to explore the henge and stone circle at nearby Avebury (see page 151) and the West Kennet Long Barrow, a Neolithic chambered tomb situated over the road and along a path. All three sites are part of a much larger prehistoric landscape that is linked by stone rows and cursuses (long, parallel earth banks) and extends for miles to Stonehenge.

Mountains in miniature

Silbury Hill is not the only mysterious man-made mound in the UK. There are a surprising number scattered all over the country. Frequently tucked away, concealed by trees and bushes, they are worth seeking out if you can locate one. Although they are often listed as motte and bailey castles, their purpose could also have been religious. Known as 'tumps', they weren't built as places to enter: none have chambers inside and few have any remains from burials either inside or on the summit. Instead, it is most likely that they were places to ascend, to get closer to the gods, to give thanks for the harvest or to offer a sacrifice.

In his book *The Old Straight Track*, Alfred Watkins suggests that tumps in Herefordshire, including those at Huntington, Oldcastle and Capler Camp, were sited at intersecting points in networks of ley lines crossing the land. Some, such as the tump in the outskirts of Lewes, have spiral paths leading to the top. This tump is described in detail in *The Druid Way* by Philip Carr-Gomm, who also points out that tumps weren't confined to Britain. They can also be seen, for example, in Holland, and in Sillustani, a pre-Incan cemetery, near the shores of Lake Titicaca in Peru. Some believe they are inhabited by dragons.

Tai Shan (Mount Tai), China

Unlike other sacred mountains, the path to the top of Tai Shan is a stairway of 6666 steps. It is difficult to get lost, but it is still a steep ascent: the summit is 1550m high, making it the highest peak in the Shandong province. Tai Shan is the most revered of the five sacred mountains of China (the others are Heng Shan, Hua, Heng and Song) and has attracted pilgrims for centuries. It is also the most visited: millions of people make the ascent every year.

Along the route to the summit are temples, shrines and inscribed stones. These serve as reminders of the mountain's spiritual importance, particularly to Taoists who believe in living in harmony with the Tao (the Way) by balancing yin (feminine) and yang (masculine) forces. One Taoist deity is the Jade Emperor, who is thought to inhabit the mountain. His temple stands at the very top.

Be prepared for crowds Many visitors climb through the night to see the sun rise in the east the following morning. It will be crowded whatever time of day you choose. It is a steep and sometimes tough climb and will take around six hours to reach the Jade Emperor's Temple.

Uluru, Central Australia

The mighty sandstone rock Uluru, which looms above the plains of the Uluru-Kata Tjuta National Park, has long had deep spiritual significance for Australia's indigenous Aboriginal people. They believe that it was created by their Dreamtime ancestors and hardened into stone when the Dreamtime ended. It is central to the beliefs of Pitjantjatjara, Yankunytjatjara and Anangu tribes and there are many myths and stories associated with it, along with traditional ceremonies that have taken place for over 10,000 years.

One of the most recognisable, and photogenic, landmarks in the world, Uluru has become a major tourist destination. It looks most spectacular at sunset when oxidation on the surface of the grey sandstone rock catches the light and turns it a fiery orange-red, but its bulk and deeply furrowed surface is impressive at any time of day.

Also in the Park is Kata Tjuta (the 'Many-headed Mountain'): a group of thirty-six domed rocks that the Anangu Aborigines believe is the home to spirit energy from the Dreaming. Much less visited than Uluru, although equally powerful, it is a more peaceful place to spend time.

Appreciate it from the ground Respect the wishes of the Aboriginal people and stay on the ground. Climbing the monument is not permitted, and, anyway, treating it as a bucket-list destination to be conquered is counter to the spirit of the place. Instead, walk around it on the flat dirt path and soak up its atmosphere, checking in with the spirits of the ancestors that occupy it.

A mindful journey to a mountain

Looking across a landscape, or over a city, towards a mountain can stir up feelings of yearning – as though the mountain is calling out to you to discover and explore it. Its scale and age make it seem as if it has wisdom to offer. No wonder mountains have been considered sacred for as long as we have lived among them.

To begin to understand a mountain, you have to walk it. No other method will reveal as much. There are two ways to do this: you can scale the summit or you can walk around the mountain's base, in the Tibetan tradition. Alternatively, you could simply ramble along its paths without any particular direction in mind. The mountain is the destination after all. If you aren't near a mountain or it isn't easy to climb one, then a small hill – chosen carefully for its meaning to you – will do just as well. There are several ways to walk a mountain.

To the top

- Before you start your ascent, find a stone and hold it in your hand. Express your intention to yourself. It could simply be to get to know the mountain better and to enjoy the walk, or you could ask the mountain for guidance – either along your route or in life.
- Either pocket the stone or replace it where you found it with a thank you.
- Start to walk steadily. It may not be possible to keep up a rhythmic pace – you might have to scrabble across scree or scramble through bracken – but try to choose your steps slowly and thoughtfully.

- Be aware of your senses. There will be different colours to see, from the earthy tones beneath your feet, to the bright hues of wild flowers and the greys, blues and white of the sky. What plants, trees and birds can you identify? What fragrance can you smell – not just the flowers, but what other scents are being carried in the air? There may be a bonfire burning in the distance, you might detect the scent of an animal close by, or the distinctive fragrance of a pine tree.
- When you reach the summit, allow feelings of achievement to subside (remember, a mountain is not there simply to be conquered) and find a place to sit.
- Look around at the land that surrounds you. How far can you see? What is on the horizon, and what colours are in the sky?
- Visualise light beaming out from you to all quarters of the Earth: to the north, south, east and west. This is a druidic way of sending out love, light and healing to all beings.
- Thank the mountain and ask it to serve as a guide on the way down.
- Walk steadily back to base, savouring every moment as you do so and being grateful for spending time in such a lovely place.

Around the base

This approach can be tricky on mountains that aren't designated pilgrimage routes: footpaths probably won't obligingly circle the base and landowners might have something to say about you traipsing across their fields. You could try it on smaller, man-made hills like Silbury, though, or, if not near a mountain, you could walk around something entirely different: a stone picked up from the slopes of one and brought home, perhaps.

Circumambulation (walking around something) is a powerful spiritual walking practice and can be applied to many things. Circling an object creates a bond with it – each time you repeat the circuit, you notice new things. Moving around it, you pay homage, showing it reverence and a willingness to learn more about it.

A word of caution: Mountains can be dangerous places with unpredictable weather and unexpected perils. A storm can blow up out of nowhere, mist can descend obscuring the path and darkness comes quickly. Remember to tell someone where you have gone and at what time, and check weather reports before you go. Don't disregard warnings, and remember to wear appropriate footwear and clothing.

4

The Wisdom of Trees

*Few journeys have the power to uplift as the one
following a winding path through a forest.*

It was a baking hot Sunday during the school holidays and I
was in limbo. Kicking my heels around the house, I waited for
the weeks to pass before I went to university. In my boredom
and listlessness, I took a book about local history from my
father's bookshelf, expecting it to be about Civil War skir-
mishes or Tudor buildings – things that, at the time, did not
interest me. Leafing through the pages, though, I came across a
paragraph about a tree. Surprised that a tree should be worthy
of a mention, I read on.

The tree in question was a yew and it grew in a churchyard
a few miles from our house in the village of Much Marcle,
Herefordshire. There were a few noteworthy things about this

tree. One was its age: it was more than 9m in circumference, which meant that it was at least a thousand years old. How could anything live that long, I wondered. Also of significance was that it was hollow – so hollow that there was a seat inside it where you could perch, surrounded by actual tree. My boredom subsided. I wanted to go and find this tree and sit in it.

Fortunately, my parents, fed up of my hanging around the house, agreed to drive me there, and the three of us set off to find it. The yew wasn't hard to locate – like many yews it was beside a church. We parked on the street nearby – I was a teenager so reluctant to walk anywhere – and went to look at the yew.

It was extremely wide, shaped like a fat-bellied bottle, and some of its lower branches were propped on iron supports. And it was indeed hollow.

At the time I didn't realise that this was an ancient tree, one with status and wisdom imbued in its furrowed bark. I saw it as more of a novelty. It was, in fact, older than the thirteenth-century church, St Bartholomew's, that it grew beside. I also didn't know that, because they have been around forever, and live so long – longer than most things on earth – and because they have an almost supernatural ability to regenerate, yews have been held sacred by various cultures for centuries. These include the Celts, Greeks, Romans and North American Indians, who consider them a symbol of rebirth.

My father and I went and sat inside. It was good to get out of the sun and rest in the cool, earthy heart of the yew. It felt safe in there, sitting with my dad, surrounded by crinkly wood, peeping out at the world. It smelt warm and familiar, like my father's tin of pipe tobacco. The nerves I had felt about the next stage in my life – leaving home, living in a city – eased. My mother took a photograph of us. As always, my father was frowning, anxious that she was pressing the wrong button. She didn't though: the photograph came out just fine. I still have it and consider it to be my first encounter with a remarkable tree. It is also a reminder of my now late father, when the world, for a moment or two at least, was a safe place and I felt protected.

The wonder of woods

Few journeys have the power to uplift as one following a winding path through a forest. On a spring day new leaves are revealed, backlit by the low sun – lime green and paper-thin – and there may be bluebells to see or ferns uncurling. In summer the sun sifts through the canopy, providing dappled shade, and in autumn twigs and bracken crackle underfoot as leaves fall and mushrooms balloon from rotten trunks. In winter a wood is a world of dramatic silhouettes, the skeleton and bark of the trees revealed. The Japanese have a word for this practice of 'forest bathing' – *shinrin-yoku*. They believe that a slow, mindful walk in the forest lowers blood pressure and reduces stress. In his book *Wildwood*, Roger Deakin suggests that entering a wood is a transformational process whereby we find ourselves, paradoxically, by getting lost.

Little wonder then, that these magical places are deeply rooted in our imaginations, generating folk tales and fairy stories, harbouring fantastic creatures and mythical beings. Tolkien's elderly, wise, talking trees, the Ents, in the forest of Middle Earth in *The Lord of the Rings*, for example, are similar to those of folklore; Hansel and Gretel get lost in the forest and captured by a witch; Lucy enters the magical forest of Narnia through the wardrobe in *The Lion, the Witch and the Wardrobe*, and Little Red Riding Hood is pursued by a wolf through the woods.

Little wonder also that trees have been venerated in different cultures for generations. The symbol of the Tree of Life, a metaphor for creation, is widespread and represented in many religions, including Buddhism, Islam and Christianity. In Scandinavian mythology, it is known as Yggdrasil and unites the underworld with earth through root, trunk and branch. Sacred springs rose all around it.

Trees were also venerated by First Nations peoples of the Pacific Northwest coast, who would look for a tree, most often a red cedar, fell it as they performed a ritual, then trim, carve and paint it. The carvings, which include fish, people, plants and birds, would represent ancestors, events and legends. The pole, known colloquially as a totem pole, was then raised and became the centre of ritual dances.

The Celts believed that a tree was a deity in its own right, and that the first woman was a rowan tree, the first man an alder. The Ancient Greeks assigned each god his or her own tree: the oak was sacred to Zeus, the myrtle to Aphrodite. And, according to Irish folklore, a single hawthorn in the middle of a field is inhabited by fairies, with especially sacred status if it grows near a well. Druids continue to worship in sacred groves – 'clearings open to the sky' – in the heart of woodland. There is no end to the links between trees, ourselves and mythology.

With such relationships, you would imagine we would

always have valued and protected our forests, but trees are also extremely useful, providing timber for shelter, building and fuel. Our insatiable need for these has led to massive deforestation. We tend to think that modern man is responsible for the over-felling of forests, but our ancestors started the process: early Iron Age man cleared about 50 per cent of British woodland by 500 BC, and the Hopi Indians in Arizona destroyed many of their forests. Despite restoration and replanting projects now in place, there is still a tendency to take trees for granted and not to give them the respect they deserve. Pilgrimage is one way to redress the balance.

Ancient trees

A pilgrimage to an ancient tree, a wood, a forest or even a copse in a local park is good for the tree and good for the soul. Although you don't have to make an ancient tree your destination – a younger one is equally valid in its own way – these wise and venerable beings feel worthier of the trip.

Fortunately, in Britain we are never far from a tree. As well as those found in the country, they are all around us in cities and towns, providing shade from the sun, inhaling CO_2 and exhaling oxygen and water, providing habitat for birds, insects and other wild creatures. They are the heroes of our land, but are largely unsung until they are felled by councils or developers, when we feel a pang of bereavement and loss.

A tree reaches 'ancient' status depending on its species. If a willow or birch lives to 150 years, it is ancient, but this is merely middle aged for an oak. Oaks and sweet chestnuts live for centuries before they are officially 'ancient', and the oldest yews go on for even longer, some reaching between 4000 and 5000 years. In the Yosemite National Park, California, one giant sequoia called General Sherman is estimated to be between 2300 and 2700 years old, and the largest single living organism in the world. That is a tree to treat with respect.

The UK has more ancient trees than the whole of Europe, and their age and presence makes any one of them a fitting destination for a pilgrimage. Although they have been with us for centuries, you won't find any marked on Ordnance Survey maps and they are rarely recorded in historical documents. Fortunately, they are easy to spot in a landscape: they are generally shorter and more squat – the result of coppicing and pollarding early in their lives. Frequently they have a hollow trunk, areas of bark and limb decay, and limbs that grow downwards. Some are 'witness trees', a term that originally meant they were planted to mark boundaries, but which has come to signify a tree that has seen many things and is 'a repository for the past'.

In England and Wales an ancient woodland is defined as an area that has been continuously wooded since 1600; in Scotland since 1750. Ancient woodland has many unique and precious features. Its relatively undisturbed soil encourages communities of plants and animals. Many have spectacular displays of bluebells and wood anemones in spring, abundant species of fungi, wild garlic and many other wild flowers.

Although many ancient trees are found in woodland, many are not and have survived as solitary specimens in village greens, fields, commons, grounds of stately homes, churches or in hedgerows. These trees are often admired for their longevity – chances are that they will outlive all of us – and for their beauty. They are good to hang out with. You get the feeling they have a lot to teach us.

A cautionary note: forests, especially at night, can also be places of terror, as anyone who has seen *The Blair Witch Project* or *Evil Dead* knows only too well. Film makers are keen to tap into our fear of their wild and elemental nature, where things wait in the shadows ready to pounce. Even woodland creature Mole in *Wind in the Willows* by Kenneth Grahame got the fear:

'Then the pattering began ... As he lay there panting and trembling, and listened to the whistling and the patterings outside, he knew it at last, in all its fullness, that dread thing which other[s] ... had encountered here and known as their darkest moment ... – the Terror of the Wild Wood.'

Be alert as you walk but try not to be spooked by fear-whipping film makers and scare-mongering children's authors. Woodland is mostly a delightful place to spend any amount of time.

Sea henge: risen from the depths

In 1998, a mysterious ring of tree stumps was revealed as a tidal surge swept sand from Holme beach in North Norfolk. Buried beneath the sand for 4000 years, the fifty-five split oak trunks circled around a huge, upended oak tree stump at the centre. Quickly labelled 'sea henge' because of ▶

its resemblance to Stonehenge, the circle, and the great upside-down tree at its heart, baffled archaeologists. Perhaps, we can imagine, it was meant to resemble the tree of life and planted as a link between the earthly realm and the underworld. The oak was sacred to the Druids, and other timber circles, now lost, were made from it, so the choice of oak could be revealing.

Originally constructed on saltmarsh, the circle gradually, over the centuries, became buried in peat and then, with rising sea levels, sand and sea. This conserved the stumps and kept them hidden from view until the storms revealed them to an amateur archaeologist, John Lorimer, as he was out beachcombing.

Unfortunately, sea henge is no longer a mysterious site emerging from the shallows of the East Anglian coast. Any modern pilgrim wanting to see the ancient oak stump and timber posts must travel to the Lynn Museum in King's Lynn, Norfolk, where they were taken for preservation and where they still draw pilgrims and the curious.

Pilgrimages to wise and noble trees

Each species of tree has its own character, whether it's the elegant and breezy ash or the stout and dependable oak. Once you know the characteristics of a few native trees, you'll be able to assess which one suits your temperament and head off to make its acquaintance.

Yew (*Taxus*)

How you will know it Look for a dense, dark-green tree of indeterminate shape. As it's evergreen, it keeps its needle-like leaves all-year round. Birds like to feast on its red berry-like fruits called 'arils'. It has upswept branches and reddish-brown bark.

A potted profile Yews can live to a mind-boggling age: some UK yews are older than Stonehenge. Their incredible longevity and almost supernatural ability to regenerate have made them objects of veneration and a symbol of rebirth and everlasting life. When Christians co-opted pagan sites to build churches, they also co-opted the yew trees that grew there and were considered sacred by native Britons.

Churchyards are still the best places to find an ancient yew, many of which are living shells – yews hollow out as they age – but you can also find amazing examples clipped into topiary shapes in stately homes. Here are some examples.

- **The Crowhurst Yew, Church of St George, Crowhurst, Surrey** Said to be 4000 years old, this must be the oldest yew in the country. With its vast girth and tangle of branches, it looks like something from Middle Earth. Its elderly branches are supported on wooden poles and its hollow trunk has been fitted with a wooden door. The perfect place to tuck yourself away.
- **L'If de l'église, Church of Saint-Ursin, Saint-Ursin, France** With a girth of almost 10m,

this is a mighty and ancient tree and is sited beside the entrance to the Norman church. Also hollow enough to immerse yourself in.

- **The Nevern Yews, St Brynach Church, Nevern, Wales** Not ancient (though still around 700 years old), but renowned because one of them 'bleeds' a blood-red sap, which has had several legends attributed to it.

- **Ankerwyke Yew, near Wraysbury, Berkshire** A solid chunk of tree that resembles a piece of molten rock. All sorts of historical happenings are said to have occurred here, including Henry VIII's courtship of Anne Boleyn. As well as sitting inside its hollow trunk, you can actually climb up inside it and get to its very core.

- **Shugborough Yew, Shugborough Hall, Staffordshire** Believed to be the widest tree in Britain, and with the largest crown, this yew has reached a circumference of 175m and is still spreading, engulfing other trees around it. A tree to walk around or burrow into.

- **Ancient yew, St Coeddi's Church, Fortingall, Perthshire, Scotland** This tree has its own walled enclosure within the village churchyard to protect it from souvenir hunters. Another very elderly tree, it is estimated to be between 2000 and 5000 years old.

Find a yew near you at ancient-yew.org

Oak (*Quercus*)

How you will know it It will greet you with open arms – oaks like to spread sideways given half the chance. It will have gnarly bark with many ridges and fissures, easily recognisable lobed leaves that resemble paw prints, and a cloud-like, rounded outline.

A potted profile The oak is the one tree that most of us recognise. Its deep roots and sheer bulk mean that it can withstand whatever the weather throws at it, and its generous canopy attracts many different insects and birds. Its timber is hard and tough, making it a valuable resource for shipbuilding in the past, and for house-building and tool-making in the present.

In the Classical world the oak was regarded as the Tree of Life, with its roots penetrating into the Underworld and it branches soaring towards heaven. In Scandinavia it was seen as the tree of Thor, the thunder god. Dense forests of oak covered most of northern Europe at one time. Druids practised their religion in oak groves and many of these became sites for Christian churches. Folklore surrounding the oak suggests that it has curative powers (walking around it and asking for the ailment to be carried away by a bird was considered enough to heal) and in Cornwall, driving a nail into its trunk was said to cure toothache.

Oaks are particularly prone to lightning strikes because they are deep-rooted and often stand alone. Mistletoe, a plant revered by Druids, was said to grow on oak as a result of lightning striking there.

A recent survey by the Woodland Trust revealed that England has more ancient oak trees than other European countries, despite extensive deforestation. Tree historians discovered 1200 previously unknown, but still surviving, medieval and Tudor oaks, making the grand total 3400. Here are some of them.

- **The Bowthorpe Oak, near Bourne, Lincolnshire** What could be England's oldest oak tree (estimated at over 1000 years old) sits sturdily on the private land of Bowthorpe Park Farm. The tree feels friendly and welcoming and visitors are invited to sit inside it (there are seats) and marvel at its longevity.
- **Whiteleaved Oak, near Eastnor, Herefordshire** Many mystical associations radiate from this stout and elderly tree. It is still used in druidic ceremonies and offerings are tied from its branches. Leave your own, then sit and contemplate the view of the Malvern Hills rolling away before you.
- **Major Oak, Edwinstone, Sherwood Forest, Nottinghamshire** These days, the collapsing branches of this 800-year-old tree are propped up on poles, but back in the day they allegedly sheltered Robin Hood and his merry men.
- **Tree of life, Audubon Park, New Orleans, Louisiana, United States** Situated in what was once a plantation, this Southern Live Oak or *Quercus virginiana* has expansive boughs to embrace you and is draped with Spanish moss

to further boost its mystery. It is one of several Live Oaks in the park, including some of the largest in the state.

Hawthorn (*Crataegus*)

How you will know it In spring it is smothered in milk-white blossom, but don't be fooled by this frothiness – beneath it lie sharp thorns up to 3cm in length. Its fruits, called 'haws' are deep red. Solitary hawthorns often strike dramatic angles on wind-buffeted spots, others bunch together in hedgerows: its impenetrable spiky and dense foliage make it the perfect plant for hedging.

A potted profile Also known as the May as it flowers during that month (although in recent years it has been flowering earlier), the hawthorn has played a central part in Beltane (May Day) festivities for centuries and has many associations with magic and ritual. In Ireland, it is considered the tree most likely to be inhabited by fairies and is seen as a portal to their world. If a hawthorn is cut down or damaged, you run the risk of angering them. You will often find hawthorns at sacred sites, such as holy wells, where they are festooned with clootie rags and ribbons and other votive offerings.

- **The Glastonbury Thorn, Glastonbury, Somerset**
  Over the years, many pilgrims have made their way to this tree on Wearyall Hill to the southwest of Glastonbury. It is an important site for Christians as, according to legend, Joseph of

Arimathea (the man responsible for the burial of Jesus) left Jerusalem after the crucifixion and travelled to Britain. He struck his staff into the ground and it rooted, flowering twice a year – once at Christmas and once at Easter. It has been vandalised twice, most recently in 2010, but cuttings were taken and the tree grew again. It is also a sacred site for pagans. (For more on Glastonbury, see page 119.)

- **Hethel Old Thorn, Hethel Church, Hethel, near Wymondham, Norfolk** Also linked with Joseph of Arimathea, this is one of oldest hawthorns in the country and has existed since the thirteenth century. Huge, shaggy and untamed, it also goes by the name of the Witch of Hethel.

- **The Fairy Tree, Ennis, Ireland** Such is the reverence for the hawthorn in Ireland that the new road from Limerick to Galway was routed around this tree. Tradition had it that it was the rallying point of fairies, and it was agreed that no traffic should pass within 5m of its trunk. It now sits behind a protective fence.

- **Wishing Tree, Ardmaddy, Argyll and Bute** The bark of this almost dead tree has been studded with hundreds of coins, each representing a wish. Unfortunately, the coins have contributed to its ailing, so instead tie a clootie rag on one of the few surviving boughs.

Ash (*Fraxinus*)

How you will know it The ash is tall and straight, reaching up towards the sky with branches that sweep upwards at the tips. It has six to eight oval leaflets in pairs along each leaf stem and winged fruits or 'keys' in late summer. Its buds are velvety black. Ash wood used to be harvested by coppicing mature trees, which would grow back producing several new shoots. This accounts for the stumpy, swollen nature of some older trees.

A potted profile The ash is the last tree to wake up in spring, with leaves appearing long after the others. When it does, its light, airy canopy encourages woodland flowers to grow beneath it. Because of its tall elegance, it is considered by some to be the feminine counterpart to the oak, although in Norse mythology it was Yggdrasil, the tree of existence, from whose roots man was formed. It has associations with healing and enchantment – Gandalf carries an ash staff in *The Lord of the Rings* and he should know. Here are some notable ash trees.

- **Clapton Court, Crewkerne, Somerset** At 500 years old, this is the oldest ash in England. Its enormous trunk has a girth of over 8m at its widest point.
- **Ash Dome, Ffestiniog valley, North Wales** Sculptor David Nash cleared a patch of ground in a secret location and created this 9m-wide circle of twenty-two trees in 1977. As they grew, he trained them into a vortex-like

shape. Beautiful to look at in photographs but impossible to find, so best for a desktop pilgrimage!

- **The Gordon Castle Ash, Fochabers, Scotland** This 250-year-old tree was felled in 2010 after being damaged by a storm. Cuttings were taken, however, and a new tree now grows close to the site of the old.
- **White ash, George Washington Victory Trail, West Trenton, New Jersey, USA** Sitting beside the road alongside overhead power lines, this monumental tree was planted in 1675 and has reached a height of 24.5m.

Where to find ancient woodland in the UK

- **Wistman's Wood, Two Bridges, Princetown** This magical oak woodland on Dartmoor is lush and enchanted. Oaks, stunted and gnarled by moorland winds, drip with epiphytic ferns, and granite boulders are festooned with mosses and lichens. The Dart river winds away below.
- **Kingley Vale, West Stoke, near Chichester, Sussex** The twisted yews in this woodland on the South Downs are dark and mysterious. Burial mounds are tucked away in the wood, which is Europe's largest yew forest and includes a grove of veteran trees.
- **Queen's Wood and Highgate Wood, Highgate, North London** Proof that ancient woodland

exists in the city, this oak and hornbeam wood in North London is six miles from the City. Among the trees, you will find the scarce Wild Service Tree, and the forest floor has a large population of wood anemone, buttercup, wood sorrel and St John's wort.

- **The Woodland Trust's Ancient Tree Inventory**
  This survey maps the oldest and most important trees in the UK – 160,000 so far – and encourages you to add any you find:
  ati.woodlandtrust.org.uk

A mindful journey through the forest

Once you have selected your tree and know where to find it, the time has come to make your pilgrimage. As always, the journey is as important as the destination, and shouldn't be hurried. Before you set foot in the forest, think about why you are there and what you hope to gain. It may mean nothing significant; sometimes a walk in the company of trees is enough in itself.

- Pause for a moment before you walk into the wood. Gateways are important in pilgrimage, marking the moment you leave the everyday and start your journey. The first steps into a wood, through its portal of interlaced branches, can feel like entering a different world.
- As you walk beneath the trees, breathe deeply, inhaling the humus-rich aromas of the forest

floor, the smell of pine needles and scent of wet tree trunks.

- Stop every so often and listen: you will hear the whisper of the wind as it moves through the canopy, the rustle of small creatures scurrying through leaves and twigs, and the varied and melodic songs of different birds. How many different birds' songs can you hear?
- Your path may not be direct: there are many tracks through a forest and plenty of crossroads. Keep alert, though, and you won't get lost for long.
- Look all around you and really notice what you see: twisted roots emerging from banks, mushrooms erupting from the tree trunks, ferns unfolding from mossy banks, wildflowers sprinkled on the forest floor, mustard-coloured lichen on bark and stones. Sit down on a log or tree stump and drink it all in before walking steadily on towards your destination.

And when you get there ... The path you have chosen – whether it's a walk through a wood or forest, or a stroll through a park – has led you to a special tree. Now what do you do? The biggest mistake is to rush away. A tree is in no hurry and neither are you. It's time to get to know one another.

- **Say hello.** It would be rude not to. Give your tree a stroke or, even better, a hug. This not only connects you with the tree, it gives you a sense of how old it is: the wider its girth, the more elderly the tree.

- **Sit down beside it**. Few things are as peaceful and restorative as sitting under the boughs of an ancient tree, resting your back on its sturdy trunk, listening to the rustle of its leaves. It's the best way to get a sense of the tree's roots anchoring it deep into the earth, its branches stretching out to the sky. Many old trees also have hollow trunks – the perfect place to immerse yourself and activate the senses.
- **Notice your breath**. Be aware of the air coming in and out of your body. Place your feet on the ground and imagine you are a tree and that your roots are growing out from the soles of your feet. With each breath, visualise your roots growing deeper into the earth.
- **Picture a bright light** entering the crown of your head, passing through your body and along your roots. When you breathe in imagine the white light flowing through you. When you breathe out, see this light taking all your anxieties and flushing them out into the earth.
- **Fill yourself with comfortable feelings**. Bring to mind a favourite person or event, or just open yourself to your beautiful surroundings.
- **Release your creativity.** There is a likelihood that the muse will come upon you, in which case, have a notebook ready. This could be the

time for a poem or a drawing – but don't feel you
have to do anything. Sitting quietly is enough.

- **Climb into its lower branches** if it's safe
  and permissible. Once you have clambered
  up into your tree, you will wonder why you
  haven't done it before. From your leafy lookout,
  the world will seem different: you'll feel
  adventurous and daily worries will diminish.
  Oak, ash, cedar and some types of pine tend to
  have the best shape for ladder-like ascents.
- **Leave a gift.** Say thank you to your tree for
  the time you have spent together. If it is a holy
  tree, it may already be decked with clootie rags.
  Leave one yourself or tuck an offering into the
  bark, making sure it won't harm the tree or
  create any litter.

How to tell if a tree is really ancient

When you arrive at your tree and have got to know it, you
may be curious about how old it actually is. Ancient trees
are hard to date as, of course, no one wants to cut them
down to count the rings. In her book *Hidden Histories*,
Mary-Ann Ochota suggests hugging it. This sounds daft
until you learn that the easiest way to measure the tree's
girth is to do so around its narrowest part – its waist –about
1.5m from the ground. Your arm span is roughly the same ▶

as your height, and, based on a fingertip-to-fingertip arm span of 5ft, this gives you a rough measure. If you can't reach around the trunk on your own, gather some other pilgrims and join hands. This will also give you a chance to hug a tree without feeling foolish by declaring that it's a scientific investigation.

Trees may be ancient when they reach:

- Ash: two pilgrims hugging it
- Beech: two pilgrims hugging it
- Oak: three pilgrims hugging it
- Sweet Chestnut: four pilgrims hugging it

5

Gardens for the Soul

A pilgrimage is a way of discovering,
listening and responding to the *genus loci* –
the spirit – of a garden.

Gardens may not be the most obvious place for a pilgrimage. There is a tendency to think of them as a substitute for a wild, natural landscape, and somehow not worthy as a destination – more of places to go for a day trip, a stop off for tea and cake, than a sacred place worthy of a pilgrimage. But this is to do them a disservice. No matter how big or small a cultivated patch is, it is always a connection – a pathway – to the earth. Visiting a garden is a way to bridge our growing separation from the land.

Every garden has its own spirit and *genus loci*, which varies from plot to plot, country to country. A pilgrimage is a way of discovering, listening and responding to it. Find a garden that speaks to you, for whatever reason – you may admire the gardener who created it, or it could be a rose garden in a park that your grandmother loved or something else altogether.

In Classical antiquity, gardens were designed to replicate sacred landscapes. Mountains and rivers were created in miniature and became places of pilgrimage and veneration for those who could not travel to the real thing. They were also as near as it was possible to get to heaven. Walled gardens where fountains played and trees were heavy with ripe fruit were little patches of paradise on earth.

Throughout history to the present day, gardens have been a place of sanctuary, nourishment and tranquillity – reason enough to make one the focus of a pilgrimage, even if you are not a gardener yourself. And if you still have reservations about visiting this tamed version of nature, remember that, in the end, the wild will return. None of us own a garden, we are merely its custodians until nature reclaims it and it takes on a life of its own once more.

Some gardens capture the imagination more than others. Unvisited but legendary, they are places of mythic loveliness, abundant with flowers, trees and birds – a promise of paradise. Often celebrated for their innovation or influence, they are written about in magazines and books, or lovingly filmed on TV programmes, described in terms that make you yearn to see them yourself.

Rousham Gardens in Oxfordshire was one such place for me. An enthusiastic amateur gardener, I had read an account of it by garden designer Dan Pearson that described it as 'restful, spacious, timeworn and beautifully paced'. Situated on the banks of the River Cherwell, with pools, wooded paths, a serpentine rill and undulating lawns peppered with Classical statues, it sounded almost Arcadian – somewhere lost and out of reach.

The garden was created by William Kent, the great eighteenth-century landscape gardener, and it has hardly changed since it was built. This is largely because the same family has lived there for generations and, respectful of its original layout, has made very few alterations all that time. Kent's intention was to create a garden that took visitors on a tour around a picturesque landscape, enticed to step ever onwards by a glimpse of a statue, the sound of water or the sight of a temple on the brow of the hill. This sounded like a mini pilgrimage, and was all the more reason to visit.

Despite all of that, however, the months rolled on and I still hadn't got around to going. There were always other drearier claims on my weekend: food to buy, DIY to master. Then one Friday, I decided that the time had come. We would ignore mundane chores, I told my partner, Max, take a picnic and a Thermos and go.

It was the height of a hot summer when we set off along the lanes of Oxfordshire towards Rousham, bowling along in my ancient car like Mr Toad. As Rousham is privately owned, tucked away and has no café or gift shop, it's not that well known or visited. You approach along a long drive lined with elderly trees and cattle slowly munching the grass. The house sits back behind a row of cottages, grand and handsome, but it was not what we had come to see. Tickets for the garden were paid for by putting coins into a machine. No one was around to sell us a guide or a membership. It felt like we had the place to ourselves.

We walked across a lawn, then, as we turned a corner around the house, the garden opened out before us. Kent was an advocate of 'borrowed landscape'; rather than enclosing a garden or designing it in a style that was contrary to its surroundings, he believed that a garden should connect with the landscape. A wide-open view did exactly that – it was impossible to see where the garden ended and the countryside began. Gentle hills rolled away into the distance and a folly drew our eyes beyond the boundary.

Passing a statue of a lion savaging a horse, we continued into the garden. The journey, though short, was epic. Determined to follow the circuit as Kent intended, we discovered an arcaded terrace, a path shaded by yew trees, a temple, a cascade and a wriggling rill, which led to a still, octagonal pool. Classical statues – of a dying gladiator, Venus and Apollo – surprised us as we walked.

We stopped to eat our lunch beside the pool, with the River Cherwell rippling past just out of sight. Lying in the long grass with only the sound of water and drowsy bees to disturb the peace was a little moment of heaven. This is what the promise of a garden is all about and why the best ones are always worth taking the time and effort to visit.

Japanese sacred gardens

In the West there is a tendency to ignore rocks and dismiss their immobile, unchanging nature (unless you are a stone seeker, see page 16). They vanish into the background and become part of the landscape. In Imperial China, however, rocks were central to Buddhist beliefs. Thought to harbour chi – the vital energy that animates the world – being close to one was beneficial to health and wellbeing, especially if the rock was an unusual shape. Consequently, Imperial gardens often featured rocks, which were also used to symbolise sacred mountains, considered to be the centre of the universe.

In Japan, rocks were also venerated and, according to Shinto beliefs, inhabited by gods and spirits. When Buddhism reached Japan from China, it brought its garden-making principles with it. This led to a style of dry gardening known as *kare-sansui*, and first appeared in an eleventh-century gardening manual called the *Sakuteiki*. These dry gardens were defined as places 'without pond or stream where one arranges rocks' and became the framework for Zen gardens.

The master of Zen gardens was a wandering priest called Musō Soseki. In 1339, he restored the Saihō-ji Zen Buddhist Temple (also known as the Kokedera Temple) garden near Kyoto. One feature he introduced was a garden in which rocks were placed so that they appeared to tumble down a slope – a 'dry cascade' resembling water. He also 'planted' rocks so that they could 'grow'. Amazingly, they did: the moist environment and filtered light passing through the bamboo and acer canopy encouraged the growth of 120 kinds of moss (*kokedera* means moss) and, over the years, the garden has become a soft, luxuriant and meditative space.

Any pilgrim visiting the garden must tread lightly on the meandering moss-covered paths so as not to do any damage. Some bridges are not walked on at all to preserve them. The number of visitors to the garden is limited and everyone is advised to meditate before entering. This encourages them to approach the garden with grace and respect – a good way to enter any garden or, indeed, any sacred place.

There are several other temple gardens to discover in Kyoto (and many others throughout Japan) but perhaps the most famous is the Ryoanji Temple. Created by an unknown designer, it is a simple rectangle of raked gravel within which are fifteen grey rocks of varying shapes and sizes, arranged in five groups. Although nothing grows here, it is an evocative miniature landscape which has been hugely influential and copied worldwide. Its symbolism and purpose remains mysterious, but it has been a place of contemplation since the sixteenth century and continues to be so.

Paradise gardens

Anyone who has ever watched a film in which a weary band of Bedouins and camels come upon an oasis in a desert, after days of walking across the sand in the heat, can imagine that it must feel like reaching heaven. These natural and man-made pockets of lushness, with palm trees providing welcome shade from the unrelenting sun, are a place to rest as parched throats are quenched and fruit is picked. Pools and fountains cool the air and lower the temperature. They are welcome, restorative places for any weary traveller. They are paradise.

The word 'paradise' derives from the Persian word *pairi-daeza* and means 'walled garden'. There are many references to the four gardens of Paradise in the Qur'an, and, as a result, this quadrilateral layout was replicated in Persian gardens. It is also reminiscent of descriptions of the Garden of Eden in Genesis, which is described as having a central spring that fed four rivers.

Known as a *charbagh* garden (*char* is four, *bagh* means garden), the layout was rectangular with the garden divided into four parts by paths or canals within a walled enclosure. A central fountain and flowing water were other key elements, and many had (and still have) pavilions to sit beneath to catch a cooling breeze.

When Persia was conquered by Arabs in the seventh century, displacing indigenous faiths with Islam, the Arabs adopted Persian garden design concepts, while adding some ideas of their own. These medieval Islamic gardens were similarly enclosed and followed the same rigid, formal, four-part pattern. Four channels of water flowed from a central spring, a reference to the four directions (north, south, east, west). Four is a magic and holy number and it, and its sub-divisions, occur frequently in Islamic gardens. As well as running water, still pools were constructed to reflect the sky, and fruit trees such as pomegranates and figs were planted. The aim was to create an earthly Paradise.

The *charbagh* garden was introduced to India by the Muslim Mughals, who ruled much of the country from the sixteenth to the nineteenth century. The Taj Mahal, with its 300-square-metre garden divided into four quarters of sixteen sunken flower beds, is probably the best-known example. With avenues of trees and fountains leading to the great white-domed Mausoleum (the tomb of Mumtaz Mahal, the wife of the Mughal emperor Shah Jahan, who died in childbirth), it is an earthly vision of heaven.

The Shalimar Gardens in Lahore, Pakistan also offer a glimpse of an earthly utopia. Built in 1641, also during the reign of Shah Jahan, as a place to entertain guests, the gardens have the most elaborate series of fountains (410 in total), pools and cascades of any Mughal garden. Enclosed within brick walls and intricate fretwork panels, its square terraces and marble paths are softened by many different varieties of trees and flowering plants.

In Spain, the Court of Lions in the Alhambra in Granada, with its central fountain and four rills connecting a further four fountains, is similarly heavenly, as are the gardens of the royal palace Alcazar in Spain with their channels, fountains, pools and productive orchards and vegetable beds.

Gardens incorporating the harmony and symmetry of Islamic gardens continue to be bulit. Highgrove Royal Gardens in Gloucestershire has a Carpet Garden inspired by Turkish carpets and designed by Islamic gardens expert Emma Clark; and the Mughal Garden in Lister Park, Bradford, Yorkshire is built around a similar central axis, with pools and channels of water making quite a contrast to the more usual carpet bedding on the terrace above.

Pilgrimages to artists' gardens

Go on a pilgrimage to a garden made by an artist and you'll get a sense of that person and their inspirations. The choice of plants and landscaping reveals much about their life and what drove their creativity. Gardens like Frida Kahlo's in Mexico are integral to the house, which is as it was when she died and feels like she might open the door and stand beside you at any moment.

Claude Monet: Giverny, France

Monet diverted a stream and dug a pond to create this ethereal landscape of water lilies, weeping willow and wisteria. The scene with its curved Japanese bridge was the subject of some of Monet's best known and most loved paintings, and visitors can stand where he once did and try to see it through his eyes. The rest of the garden, the house and studio complete the picture. See giverny.org

Ian Hamilton Finlay: Little Sparta, Pentland Hills, South Lanarkshire, Scotland

Five acres of exposed moorland were turned into an outdoor exhibition of 270 artworks by Ian Hamilton Finlay, including his own concrete poetry and work by other artists and craftsmen. He also built two temples from outbuildings and a pool with a fountain. The result is like a physical manifestation of his creative mind. It's best to visit in June, July and August when trees and plants – designed to be integral to the work – look their best. See littlesparta.org.uk

Frida Kahlo: Caza Azul, Coyoacán, Mexico City

The central courtyard of the house with its vivid blue walls, where Frida Kahlo was born and where she died, is filled with luxuriant indigenous plants. Cacti, apricot and pomegranate trees, and spiky agave plants sit beside Mexican folk artefacts and an Aztec pyramid designed by her husband Diego Rivera. All of these elements reflect the character and style of this influential and troubled artist. A true place of pilgrimage. See museofridakahlo.org.mx

The Bloomsbury Group: Charleston, Sussex

Many Bloomsbury acolytes visit this farmhouse near Firle to immerse themselves in the artistic household and to see their colourful and exuberant ceramics, textiles and paintings first hand. The cottage garden, created by Vanessa Bell and Duncan Grant, has wide borders filled to the brim with beautiful blooms, interspersed with sculpture, and is equally revealing. See Charleston.org.uk

Henry Moore: Hoglands, Much Hadham, Hertfordshire

The British sculptor lived here, with his wife Irina and their daughter, from 1940 until his death. As he grew better known and his work fetched higher prices, he bought more of the land around the house. The resulting 70 acres provided the perfect setting for some of his iconic bronze sculpture. Smaller pieces are displayed in his former studios. See henry-moore.org

Derek Jarman: Prospect Cottage, Dungeness, Kent

A walk along the shingle foreshore of Dungeness takes you to one of the most unexpected gardens in Britain. Spilling out around a simple black cottage, where film maker Derek Jarman lived towards the end of his life, the garden has no boundaries and plants grow in unexpected places. Anyone can walk among the frills of sea kale, the mounds of santolina, the twisted pieces of marine jetsam and bleached driftwood. It is a strange and peaceful place where the spirit of Jarman is still very much present.

Charles Jencks: The Garden of Cosmic Speculation, Dumfries, Scotland

Created by a landscape architect and theorist, the private garden of Charles Jencks is a man-made construct that references the underlying principles of nature. Swirling pools and hills carved into spirals nod to fractal, black holes and wave forms. It's an unsettling but strangely beautiful place. It opens one day a year for Maggie's cancer charity. See charlesjencks.com

Salvador Dalí: Dalí Museum-House, Portlligat, Catalonia, Spain

For over fifty years Dalí lived on and off in what had originally been a fishing hut. The house, now a museum, was extended by Dalí into labyrinthine corridors and rooms with windows of all shapes and sizes. The focus of the garden is a penis-shaped pool around which are giant Pirelli-tyre signs, huge stone eggs and a sofa in the shape of a pair of pink lips. Standard surrealist stuff, really. See salvador-dali.org

Georgia O'Keeffe: O'Keeffe Museum, Abiquiu, Santa Fe, New Mexico

Georgia O'Keeffe installed large windows into the adobe house where she lived and worked so that she could see and have a connection with the expansive landscape all around. Beyond the thick terracotta walls of the house, her garden was sparse yet productive: there was an apple tree and a walled vegetable plot. She said that she was surprised to find 'what a warming difference [a garden] can make in one's life'.

Tours by appointment. See okeeffemuseum.org

Pilgrimages to the gardens of horticultural heroes

If you are a keen gardener, chances are that you have a horticultural hero – someone whose skill with garden design or plants you admire and have been influenced by. A pilgrimage to one of their gardens is a way of paying homage to that person, to inhabit the beautiful space they cultivated, and to pick up inspiration (and a couple of plants if there is a nursery) for your own plot while you're at it. Here are five horticultural heroes.

1. Christopher Lloyd: Great Dixter, Northiam, East Sussex

Few other gardeners combined plants and colours so skilfully or with such riotous effect as Christopher Lloyd. He inherited Great Dixter, a Lutyens house with a medieval barn and eighteenth-century oast houses, from his father, Nathaniel

Lloyd, who also established the structure of the garden. Christopher died in 2006 leaving behind a world-recognised garden with, among other triumphs, an abundant and beautiful long border, a ground-breaking wildflower meadow, an exotic garden filled with banana plants and cannas, and clusters of pots brimming with unexpected plant combinations. All this is now under the stewardship of head gardener Fergus Garrett, who continues to develop and innovate. The garden reaches its peak in late summer, so head there in August and September. See greatdixter.co.uk

2. Beth Chatto: The Beth Chatto Gardens, Elmstead Market, Colchester, Essex

Any gardener who has successfully planted drought-loving plants has surely been influenced by Beth Chatto. She transformed the wasteland around her new home, bought in the 1990s, into an inspirational garden by turning the car park into a Gravel Garden (which is never watered) and a soggy ditch into a pond surrounded by bog-loving plants. She died in 2018, but the legacy of her garden, nursery, books and her dictum 'right plant, right place' continues to bring horticultural pilgrims from all over the world. See bethchatto.co.uk

3. Piet Oudolf: various gardens

The Dutch plantsman has inspired many of us to garden in blocks of herbaceous plants and grasses which drift and meld into each other – a style known as New Perennial Planting. The Oudolfs' own home and garden in the Netherlands is no longer open to the public. You can, however, step into his world of wafting perennials and shivering grasses on the High Line in New York, the Lurie Garden in Millennium Park, Chicago, or at Hauser & Wirth Garden and Gallery in Somerset.

See Oudolf.com; thehighline.org; luriegarden.org; hauserwirth.com

4. James van Sweden and Wolfgang Oehme: Federal Reserve Board Garden, Washington DC

Landscape architect James van Sweden worked with plantsman Wolfgang Oehme (who had the plant expertise) to create a style of planting that came to be known as the New American Garden. This loose and informal way of gardening favours perennial plants found on the prairies and was in distinct and deliberate contrast to the neat lawns and picket fences of suburbia. The Federal Reserve Board Garden in Washington ripples with mass plantings of native grasses and herbaceous perennials with plenty of places to sit and admire both.

5. Vita Sackville-West: Sissinghurst Castle, Kent

This hugely influential garden was created in the 1930s by Vita Sackville-West and her husband, Harold Nicolson. Designed as a series of ten rooms, including the world-famous White Garden, there is much to inspire the garden pilgrim, including the tower where Vita wrote while she looked over her horticulture creation below.

See nationaltrust.org.uk/sissinghurst-castle-garden

A mindful pilgrimage around a garden

Whichever garden has drawn you from your home, take time to get to know it by walking mindfully around it, for at least some of the time. Public gardens and parks, unlike remote countryside, can get popular, but often a short walk from the busy areas will take you to a tranquil spot.

- Like ancient sites and temples, all gardens have entrances. Find the gate and pause before going in. Notice your mood. You might have arrived hot and bothered after walking there or still feel anxious after looking for a parking space. Allow yourself time to settle and become centred.
- Think about why you have chosen that garden to visit. Is it because you admire the way it is designed and planted? Perhaps it was a special place for a family member, or the garden of someone you admire? If it is associated with a particular person, bring them to mind and invite them to accompany you on your pilgrimage.
- Park any expectations at the entrance to make room for the unexpected.
- Open your shoulders, breathe deeply and enjoy the wonderful feeling of being in a beautiful garden.
- If possible, walk around the perimeter of the garden first. This is easier, of course, with a

small domestic garden than a huge country estate. The idea is to get a feel for the spirit of the place.

- If possible, take off your shoes and socks and walk barefoot. If the weather or propriety prevents this, crouch and touch the ground with your hands. It's important to make contact with the earth.

- Make your way slowly into the garden and allow yourself to be immersed in it. Let the trees, flowers, insects and the sight of wind moving grass speak to you. Notice how the garden responds to you as you walk through it.

- Notice whatever emotion arises as you walk. Remember to be present and patient.

- Find a place to sit and end your mindful practice. Thank the garden for what it has delivered.

- Think about when you might return. Gardens are constantly changing and you need to come back to observe them at different times of the day and year. In this way you grow intimate with the place.

6

Following the Labyrinth

Seen as a tool for meditation, walking
a labyrinth's winding but purposeful path promises
to calm the mind, focus the thoughts and
bring the modern pilgrim to a place
of inner peace and strength.

A few years ago, I went to the Isles of Scilly to write a feature for
a magazine about its ancient sites. The islands bristle with prehistory: 60 per cent of the land is of archaeological importance
and the islands boast eighty-three burial chambers and numerous megaliths, so there was plenty to see and write about.

After an enjoyable day or two catching boats to the different islands, clambering over burial chambers and bagging a
couple of standing stones, I heard about a stone labyrinth on
the island of St Agnes. The other sites were fascinating and

situated on dramatic headlands and high ground with spectacular views – they were constructed at a time when the islands were all part of the same landmass, before sea levels rose and engulfed parts of it – but a labyrinth had an extra element of intrigue that was irresistible.

To reach St Agnes I caught the supper boat, which takes passengers to the Turk's Head pub to enjoy local ale and a fish supper as they watch the sun set. Dusk also felt like an appropriately magical time to make a pilgrimage to a labyrinth, so when the other passengers sauntered to the bar, I put the temptation of a pint of cider behind me and strode resolutely on. As the chatter of the pub and the light began to fade, I walked past stone cottages and clumps of agapanthus towards Troytown, the site of the labyrinth.

Many stone and turf labyrinths have the word 'Troy' in their name: it is an allusion to the defensive walls of the ancient city of Troy, which were built in a deliberately confusing and layered way to keep enemies at a distance. There is a turf labyrinth called the City of Troy near York in North Yorkshire, for example, and another at Troy Farm in Somerton, Oxfordshire. The one on St Agnes lies beyond Troytown Farm and Campsite (one of the country's most remote and appealing places to pitch a tent), along a muddy lane towards the sea. Passing campers who were gathered around campfires, talking quietly over mugs of tea, I walked further along the shoreline. At first, I couldn't spot the labyrinth. Made of pebbles and small rocks, it lies flat on the ground and is almost indistinguishable from other rocks and boulders scattered over the shoreline. The light was fading and many groups of stones held the promise of being a labyrinth until, on closer inspection, they turned out to be just a random collection. Then, just as I was getting anxious about missing the boat back to St Mary's, I looked a little further inland and spotted a pattern of concentric circles made from flat pebbles. There it was! I hurried over.

The Troytown labyrinth was rumoured to have been built in 1795 by Amor Clarke, a lighthouse keeper, to protect fishermen like himself by trapping unfavourable wind in its coils. It is a 'Classical' labyrinth (see page 122), about 5m across, with seven rings, similar to ones also found in fishing communities in Scandinavia (also with 'Troy' names, such as Trojaborg, Troborg and Trojienborg), the Baltic and White Sea coasts.

Theories abound about the original purpose of these stone labyrinths, from Clarke's wind prevention device to an aid to navigation, or trapping Norwegian *smagubbar* – evil sprites. Excavations of the labyrinth on St Agnes have shown that it was built on the site of a much older one, possibly as one element in a larger Neolithic sacred landscape. It is the only ancient stone and boulder labyrinth in the UK, although there are several turf versions. Few turf labyrinths manage to keep the same design over the centuries, however, as erosion and footfall do their damage, but this one made of pebbles, had.

As the sun slipped behind the Western Rocks on the horizon, and the wind whistled overhead, I paused for a moment to gather my thoughts and to introduce myself to the labyrinth. Then I stepped through a small gap in the pattern of pebbles. Although finding it had been a pilgrimage in itself, walking the labyrinth's path was a pilgrimage in miniature. Slowly and steadily, I was drawn closer and closer towards its heart, but every time I was almost at the centre, the path turned back on itself and I headed in the opposite direction. Needless to say, I got there in the end – one of the joys of a labyrinth is that there is only one route – and when I did, I sat down and let the peacefulness of the place settle around me. I didn't think about very much, I just looked out to sea at the waves breaking around the Western Rocks and listened to the call of the seabirds.

It was hard to get up and leave, but the wind was whipping up and I had a boat to catch. I followed the winding path out again, restored and serene, before setting off to join the others enjoying more corporeal pleasures at the Turk's Head.

The short and winding road

A walk through a labyrinth is one of the shortest but most meaningful pilgrimages you can take. Unlike a maze, with its bewildering choice of turnings, a labyrinth has one single path that leads clockwise into the centre and anti-clockwise back out again. This one-way – unicursal – route isn't direct, though: it switches back on itself as you near the centre. Just when you think you have arrived, you are propelled back towards the labyrinth's edge. Whatever twists and turns the path takes, however, you know that it will eventually take you to the centre, and then safely return you to where you started. This short walk has magic in it. It can transform thinking and transcend the everyday, which might explain why the labyrinth has existed in nearly all religious traditions all over the world since records began.

The earliest labyrinth is credited as being in the Palace of Knossos on the island of Crete, Greece. At its heart was the

Minotaur (a mythical creature, half man, half bull) who was slain by Theseus. Although no evidence of this labyrinth has been found, it appeared on ancient Cretan coins, and, much later, medieval labyrinths often represented a minotaur at their centre. Jill Purce, in her book *The Mystic Spiral* interprets the symbolism of that 'original' labyrinth as 'an initiatory hero test, the overcoming of death [the Minotaur] at the centre, and a subsequent return or rebirth into life.'

The labyrinth has become a universal and timeless symbol. It crops up around the world in multiple cultures in different times, forms and materials. It has been found in Sardinia, Peru, Arizona, Iceland, Egypt, India, Ireland, England, Scandinavia and China, among others. It has been cut from turf, made from stone boulders, carved into rock faces and created in mosaics.

Different cultures have bestowed labyrinths with various meanings and purposes. Christians walked them as a substitute for an actual pilgrimage to Jerusalem. Some involved them in courtship rituals or for initiation purposes. Others thought that a walk through a labyrinth protected them from evil spirits. Whatever the reason, a labyrinth has always been considered a spiritual journey and is packed with symbolism and metaphor.

Perhaps the best-known labyrinth is in the Cathedral of Our Lady of Chartres, France, laid out in tiles on the floor of the nave. Many medieval churches and cathedrals, especially in northern France, had labyrinths. These were often introduced to incorporate pagan beliefs into the new Christianity (and is also the reason why so many were later removed). Walking the labyrinth was a mini pilgrimage and counted as a journey to Jerusalem for those who weren't able to travel there – some were called *chemins a Jerusalem* (roads to Jerusalem). On Easter

Day, priests would dance along a labyrinth in a chain, passing a ball to each other down the line.

We are fortunate that many ancient, Roman and medieval labyrinths still exist and are waiting for us to discover them. A revival in interest in labyrinths, which began in California and has spread worldwide, has also led to new ones being created and walked, while old sites have been rediscovered and appreciated. Seen as a tool for meditation, walking a labyrinth's winding but purposeful path promises to calm the mind, focus the thoughts and bring the modern pilgrim to a place of inner peace and strength.

Once you have walked one labyrinth and experienced the restoration of equilibrium and sense of peace that they can bring (although they may also throw up questions that you will want to answer), you will want to walk another. By offering a temporary suspension of time and direction they simplify life: all you have to do is follow the path and tread carefully. As modern shamanic practitioner Mandy Pullen writes: 'Labyrinths are a way of entering inner and outer voids while having our feet firmly attached to what we are: our land, our Earth from which we spring and to which we return. They allow us to enter a state of anchored spiritual bliss, let our edges dissolve and feel our true selves within and without.'

 ## Pilgrimages to labyrinths

Although all labyrinths follow the same path, they differ in scale and design, from tiny labyrinths that can be tucked away in a pocket and traced with a finger, to the bigger versions in cathedrals designed for pilgrims to walk comfortably around, to the enormous – the 3D labyrinth that is Glastonbury Tor. There are a surprising number scattered all over the world, so a little searching will reveal one nearby. These are some of the most well known.

Cathedral of Our Lady, Chartres, France

The finest and best-known example of a medieval pavement labyrinth is in the nave of the Roman Catholic cathedral in Chartres. One of several that were laid in northern French cathedrals (there were others in Reims and Amiens cathedrals) from the twelfth to fourteenth centuries, the labyrinth has always been a popular destination for pilgrims.

Built early in the thirteenth century, it is circular in shape, divided into four quarters and has eleven circuits and seven 180-degree turns. It is likely to have been intended as a substitute pilgrimage path for those unable to travel to Jerusalem, and some pilgrims travelled its 261-m path on their knees as a form of penance or a supplication. The labyrinth is edged with 112 decorative spikes (known as 'lunations' after supposed lunar symbolism), creating a halo of decorative ornament that makes it unique.

The cathedral itself, which is a masterpiece of Gothic architecture, was an important place of pilgrimage. It houses the Sancta Camisia – a relic credited as having been the tunic worn by Mary at Jesus' birth – and the Well of Strong Saints (Puits de Sants-Forts), the grave of early martyred saints. Relics were an important element of medieval pilgrimage routes throughout Europe, promising holiness by association and the power to heal, answer prayers and to absolve sin. The tunic at Chartres was feared lost when the original Romanesque church burnt to the ground in 1195, but was subsequently discovered unharmed in the crypt. This miracle gave the site, and the new cathedral built to honour the relic, even greater importance.

Ensure the labyrinth will be visible Choose the time of your visit carefully. The labyrinth is often obscured by chairs but is uncovered every Friday during the summer months (from Lent to the end of October) from 10am to 5pm. There is also a tradition of removing the chairs on 21 June (midsummer day). Don't limit your visit to the cathedral either: outside in the garden of the Bishop's Palace (Les Jardin de l'Evêché) is another labyrinth cut from the grass in the seventeenth century and a lovely place to wander around.

Saffron Walden turf labyrinth, Essex

The Essex market town of Saffron Walden has become a must-visit destination for British labyrinth enthusiasts. Not only does it have the largest ancient turf labyrinth in the UK (and, some say, the world), but it also has a nineteenth-century hedge maze. Its Jubilee Garden bandstand has a modern, paved labyrinth and, in 2016, labyrinth expert Jeff Saward designed its Swan Meadow Maze (which includes miniature finger labyrinths) for the town's Maze Festival.

The biggest draw is still the turf labyrinth, however. Its scale (it's approximately 30m in diameter and has seventeen circuits cut as grooves into the ground, making the path about one mile long) and unusual design (it has four 'bastions' – circular protuberances – at each corner) make it unique. The earliest record of its existence dates from 1699 when it was recut, although it is probably much older. It has been restored several times since then, including in 1911 when the path was laid with bricks, which still remain. Its grassy undulations and central mound (rumoured to once have a tree growing from it) give it the appearance of a piece of contemporary land art – it looks sculpted from the ground – and it has inspired many modern artists. Its generous size makes it a comfortable place for several people to walk at once without constantly colliding or ducking out of each other's way, or for a solitary pilgrim to walk with ease for quite a long time.

Be sure to return Each journey through a labyrinth is new and plugs into a different time and space. It can be enlightening to compare experiences, noting what each visit has offered and how they have differed.

Glastonbury Tor, Somerset, England

You can see Glastonbury Tor from miles away. It stands alone, rising above the flat lands of the Somerset Levels, topped by a tower, the remains of St Michael's Church. The damp, low-lying ground surrounding it means that it is often shrouded in mist, giving it an other-worldly dimension. This is boosted by Arthurian and Christian myths and legends that also encircle the Tor, and which have long made it a pilgrimage destination for people of many different beliefs.

What is not apparent from a distance is that the sides of the Tor have been levelled into seven distinct terraces. Theories abound about how this came to be, from natural erosion to agricultural practices – could the terraces have been intended for vine growing? One man, Geoffrey Russell, however, was convinced that the Tor is a very rare thing: a 3D labyrinth.

Russell, who had spent years investigating labyrinth patterns, came to his conclusion after studying photographs of the Tor taken from the air by the Royal Air Force. He proposed that the seven terraces were the seven circuits of a Classical labyrinth and were intended for pilgrims to ascend from Hell (the entrance at the base) to Heaven (the summit), and that this 'journey through the labyrinth is for the regeneration of the soul'.

The idea that the route to the top is a ritual pathway is reinforced by the location of the Tor on the St Michael's Line (see page 25). This links different Michael shrines (often in high places) along the spine of South West England to St Michael's Mount in Cornwall. St Michael is considered the Christian successor to a pagan forebear who was a bearer of light and a slayer of dragons. All these elements combine to make Glastonbury Tor a place of magic and enchantment, and a fitting place for a labyrinth if ever there was one.

Take your time Don't be tempted to run up to the summit. The most rewarding way to approach is by steadily and mindfully following the spiral windings to the top. You will be rewarded (in fair weather) by views that stretch as far as the mountains of South Wales.

The Gotland Trojaborgs, Sweden

Stone labyrinths (called *trojaborgs* in Swedish) are peppered along the shorelines of Sweden, Norway and Finland, particularly around the Baltic Sea. Over 600 survive, made from boulders and rocks laid in a Classical design. Their position by the sea, often in natural harbours or on islands, has led to the supposition that, like the labyrinth of St Agnes in the Isles of Scilly, they were created to keep sailors safe. Up until the twentieth century, Swedish fishermen walked a labyrinth before setting sail to ensure a good catch: unfavourable winds would be snarled in the labyrinth's coils, along with evil sprites called *smagubbars*. In Finland, Lapp hunters walked labyrinths to protect themselves and their reindeer from wolves and wolverines.

The Swedish island of Gotland has forty stone labyrinths, the oldest dating back to medieval times, although many have been built since. The most famous of these is on the outskirts of the capital city, Visby. Visby was a major port, so it is likely that the labyrinth was indeed walked by fishermen before setting sail. There is also a local tradition of involving the Visby labyrinth in midsummer celebrations, and when fires are lit on a nearby hill on May Day eve to mark the arrival of spring. Stone labyrinths are also found in Iceland and Estonia, around the White Sea, and on the Kola Peninsula in Arctic Russia.

View the old and the new Look out for contemporary labyrinths as well as the older ones – several paved versions were built during the nineteenth century and later. One such is a Roman-style brick labyrinth which has been laid outside Visby Cathedral.

Know your labyrinths

Classical

This is one of the earliest forms of labyrinth and the least complicated to draw and make. Associated with the myth of Theseus and the Minotaur, this style of labyrinth appears on Cretan coins dating from around 400 BC, appears in sites across the ancient world, and is carved onto walls from Mexico to Spain, India to Ireland. Classical labyrinths usually have seven circuits, but some examples have eleven or fifteen.

Examples Troytown, St Agnes, Isles of Scilly; turf maze, Saffron Walden, Essex.

Roman

More complex than the Classical, these were made from mosaic tiles and laid in bathhouses, villas and tombs throughout the Roman Empire. Frequently square in shape, types include the double meander, where the path zig-zags twice in each corner before moving on to the next, and the complex triple meander where each quadrant contains three repeats. These sometimes had a minotaur at the centre as a nod to their Classical precedent.

Examples Cormérod, Switzerland; National Roman Legion Museum, Caerleon, Wales; Piadena, Italy.

Medieval

Towards the end of the ninth century, a monk called Otfrid took the Classical seven-circuit labyrinth and added four extra circuits. His drawing in the endpaper of his Book of Gospels became the template for dozens of twelfth and thirteenth century labyrinths, which became increasingly elaborate with the addition of decorative features.

Examples Chartres Cathedral, France, below; parish church of Batheaston near Bath (a 1985 copy of a medieval labyrinth from the abbey of St Bertin, Saint-Omer, Pas-de-Calais, France); church of San Vitale, Ravenna, Italy.

Contemporary

A revival of interest in labyrinths has led to many new ones being constructed, usually as a meditative tool and often sited in spectacular surroundings. Many are Classical and medieval in form, but other new designs with a modern flavour have appeared.

In New England, USA, 'Labyrinth Lady' Marty Cain holds workshops for people to make and walk labyrinths to harmonise with the land, Alex Champion builds 'earthworks' – 3D labyrinths and symbolic mazes – following sacred geometry principles, and Japanese artist Motoi Yamamoto creates extraordinary, intricate labyrinths from salt, which are ritually destroyed at the end of their creation and viewing, when the salt is scooped up and returned to the sea.

Examples The Labyrinth at the Edge Mountain Retreat (similar to the labyrinth at Chartres); Hogsback, Amatola Mountains, South Africa (also like Chartres); Damme Priory, Damme, Germany: a rocky labyrinth in a forest near a Benedictine Abbey; Lands End, San Francisco, California, USA: built by artist Eduardo Aguilera and overlooking the ocean and Golden Gate Bridge, below.

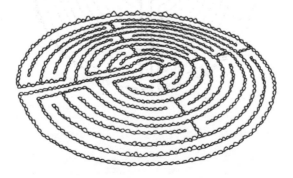

A mindful journey through a labyrinth

Walking through a labyrinth is as much about an inner pilgrimage as an outer one. A labyrinth can be a magical tool to help you answer questions, focus your mind on a goal, boost creativity, or simply to seek peace, solace or balance. Unlike a maze, which is designed to confuse, a labyrinth is all about clarity. Because there is only one route to the centre, all decisions about the way forward are taken care of, leaving your head clear to meditate, ponder or pray. It's your choice to enter a labyrinth, but once you have started walking there is only one way to go.

Following a labyrinth is different for each person who undertakes it. Rather than walk, you might choose to dance through it, like clerics in medieval France were said to do. Some pilgrims choose to divide the walk into three parts: releasing what is on their minds (the walk towards the centre); receiving any answers that come to them (standing at the centre); then returning to everyday life with their new wisdom (the walk back out).

There is no right or wrong way to walk a labyrinth, but here are some ideas that might help you along.

- Before you enter, take time to calm your thoughts and to steady yourself. Look towards the centre to give your mini pilgrimage a sense of purpose – this is where you are headed and where you will pause before you return. Now is the time to set an intention: is there something you are puzzled about or want help with? Or is there something you dream of that you want to make real? If there is, frame it into a sentence and carry the sentence in your mind as you walk.

- The looping paths of a labyrinth make it hard to hurry, which is a good thing – they are not the place for haste. Look for the entrance in the outer circle then walk slowly into the labyrinth, carefully following the path. The path ahead may look confusing, but you will soon realise that it's very easy to follow.

- Try to keep up a steady, rhythmic pace and be aware of how the path takes you first in one direction, then back on yourself and then another way forward. Focus on your intention as you walk, or use the opportunity simply to express gratitude to someone or something by repeating the words 'thank you' to yourself.

- If there are others walking the labyrinth, try to maintain a reasonable distance behind them, and if they are walking the other way and coming towards you, stand silently to one side to let them pass.

And when you get to the centre ...

- Sit, stand or even lie down, and look around you. Be ready to receive any wisdom or insights that occur. Stay as long as it feels comfortable and is practical.

- Return along the same path. This is the transition back to everyday life and is as valuable as the journey to the centre, so walk with the same care.
- After you exit the labyrinth, take time to reflect on what has just occurred. Did something happen and do you feel any different? If so, jot it down in a notebook or journal or keep it in mind as you return to daily life.

7

Icons and Idols

In former times, man-made representations of
deities were often a place of pilgrimage: young
women hoping for a child would travel to Cerne
Abbas to sit on the phallus of the enormous
chalk figure carved into a hill.

I knew about the brazen female figure carved into a corbel of
a church in Kilpeck, but my memory of it was dim. My parents
had taken me to visit the Church of St Mary and St David in
Herefordshire as a teenager as it was near where we lived.
Although at the time my mind was mostly on other things,
this carved female figure, with her legs splayed to reveal her
enlarged genitals, shook me out of my adolescent apathy.
Known as a sheela-na-gig, these carved figures are found in
medieval churches in Britain and Ireland. The boldness of the

carving in Kilpeck and the placement of it on the outside of a church wall was shocking even to a bored and not-easily-impressed teenager.

Many years later, I heard of a pilgrimage organised by the Gatekeeper Trust to the church in Kilpeck and to the Cisterician abbey church at Abbey Dore, a few miles away. The Gatekeeper Trust is a splendid organisation devoted to the simple but profound act of exploring and walking the Earth. They believe that walking mindfully on the planet 'cares for it and enhances the natural energies that flow through its crust'. These journeys, alone or with others, can involve dancing, singing and prayer, but can also be simply a walk followed by a nice sit down and a cup of tea. Whatever form they take, the intention is the same: to transform the place by making 'the atmosphere more harmonious', and to transform the inner life of the pilgrim simultaneously. As they point out: 'We live in the landscape and the landscape lives in us.'

The pilgrimage in Herefordshire began with a talk by two of the Gatekeeper Trust's members. David Furlong, an authority on earth energies, talked of how Abbey Dore is connected by a hypotenuse triangle alignment to the sacred sites of Bury St Edmunds and Glastonbury Tor. (For more on alignments, see Chapter 1.) Fiona Hopes explained how Abbey Dore occupies a pivotal point within a pattern of sacred sites within the Black Mountains and across the whole of Britain. (Alignments of earth energies are a big thing with Gatekeepers.)

After an hour or so of slides and chat it was good to get outdoors and make our way to Abbey Dore along the meandering lanes of Golden Valley. The Valley is named after the River Dore, which runs through it and the name of which is, most likely, derived from the French *d'or*, meaning 'of gold'. On a warm summer's day, the name fitted beautifully, the sun softly illuminating the gentle hills and abundant hedgerows.

Before entering the church at Abbey Dore we gathered to ask permission at the gate and then, respectfully, progressed towards the porch. The church is the only surviving structure from a large and prosperous twelfth-century monastery, whose wealth was created from sheep breeding and wool production. All of this came to an end during the Reformation and the Dissolution of the Monasteries under Henry VIII in 1537. The buildings, including the abbey, or what remained of it, were sold to local land owner John Scudamore. Scudamore dismantled what was left and removed the stone of the nave and roof of the abbey to sell. It remained a roofless ruin until 1630, when Scudamore's great-great-grandson restored it so that it functioned as a parish church. It was further restored in 1900, its final restoration, and has changed little since then.

As we walked reverentially clockwise around the abbey (more on how to approach a temple or sacred site on pages 160–62), traces of the outlying medieval monastery buildings were plain to see, indicating its original generous size and layout. Only the chancel, crossing and transepts of the original church remain, but in the chancel, a selection of roof bosses and architectural mouldings were laid out on the floor. One of these was described in the church guide as a 'foliated figure', the architectural historian's term for a green man.

There are many theories about the meaning and origins of this mask-like, half-man, half-plant figure, but this one looked benign and friendly. The beautifully carved moon-shaped face with vegetation growing from the mouth was originally a roof boss and once smiled down beatifically from the roof of the nave. It was good to meet him and we said so.

After a closing ceremony in the grounds of the now-vanished monastery, we left Abbey Dore and travelled the short distance to Kilpeck. Like Abbey Dore, the Church of St Mary and St David is enclosed by the gentle Herefordshire country-side and approached via twisting country lanes bordered by hedgerows. It feels like a secret place, although its reputation as an architectural and sculptural masterpiece makes it inter-nationally known.

Built around 1140, when the Welsh Marches (the border country between England and Wales) were prosperous, the church is adorned with a spectacular and largely undamaged series of deep-cut Romanesque carvings. Sited over a stream, which runs from under the altar down the nave, the church has a deep connection with water. This is reflected in the carv-ings, especially a Tree of Life above the door emerging from a river. Other carvings include the full range of medieval char-acters, including angels, warriors, dragons, green men, bears and snakes swallowing their own tails (a symbol known as the Ouroboros, which represents the circle of life and regenera-tion). Some of them are carved corbels (there are an impressive eighty-five altogether), which support the roof, including the much-anticipated, by me at least, sheela-na-gig.

Our little band of pilgrims split up to appreciate the build-ing and its carvings in our own individual ways. At first, I couldn't find what I was looking for, but then I saw her look-ing down at me from beneath the gable, still as startling as the first time I saw her all those years ago. Crudely carved, especially when compared to the carvings around the door, her face and body played a secondary role to her conspicuous genitalia. She certainly stood out from the other figures all around her beneath the gable.

The purpose of this seemingly vulgar figure is debatable, ranging from a fertility symbol to a warning against the dangers of lust or a protection to frighten away the devil (for more on this, see below). In more recent years, sheela-na-gigs have been reclaimed as goddess figures, and this unabashed display of female organs from the Kilpeck Whore (as she is sometimes derogatorily called) certainly delivered a powerful message about female sexuality.

Looking for icons and idols

All cultures are soaked in myths, religious stories and folk tales, and peopled with giants, dragons, gods and goddesses, fairies and sprites. These are often used to explain the inexplicable: creation, the formation of land masses, the cycles of the seasons, the existence of humanity. Some physical representations of mythical beings – carvings, statues, chalk figures – have been with us for centuries. Others are new but no less potent.

In former times, these man-made representations of deities were often a place of pilgrimage: young women hoping for a child would travel to Cerne Abbas to sit on the phallus of the enormous chalk figure carved into a hill; statues of Buddha or Hindu deities were (and still are) places of veneration and subjects of prayer; the huge Moai figures of Easter Island, carved from volcanic stone by the Rapa Nui people, were a place to go to remember the ancestors.

British folk customs are peopled by all manner of curious characters who emerge on significant days to encourage a decent harvest or to bring fertility. Among these is the sinister-looking black Obby Oss: resembling a demented and over-blown version of the child's hobby horse toy, it careens through the town of Padstow in Cornwall on May Day to bestow abundance and good luck to those it meets in its path. A local person dons the age-old costume with its frightening mask and wide, black collar and is goaded along the path by a character known as a 'teaser'. It's believed that if a young woman is caught under the Oss, she will become pregnant within a year.

In Devon on 25 May, the Earl of Rone, usually a child in a hessian costume with a scary-looking mask, is hunted through the streets of Combe Martin, 'shot' before being revived by Hobby Horses and the Fool then, finally, his costume is flung into the ocean. The tradition stems from a local legend concerning Hugh O'Neill, Earl of Tyrone, who had come from Ireland to hide in North Devon. After successfully dodging capture for several months, the Grenadiers caught up with him and killed him. Or did they? Other accounts say that he successfully made it to Spain, where he lived peacefully until his natural death.

At the Burning Man Festival in the Black Rock Desert in Nevada, California, a large wooden effigy, known as 'the Man', which takes its cue from folk customs, is burnt on the last Saturday of the event. What started as a small bonfire ritual held on a beach at the summer solstice in San Francisco has become a huge international event drawing 70,000 people. The symbolism of the blazing effigy is unexplained and foggy, but the primordial pull that draws thousands to it is all too real.

🐚 Pilgrimages to fantastic figures, beasts and deities

The Green Man

The foliage-sprouting face of the green man is an archetypal image found all over Western Europe as well as in parts of Asia and North Africa. He first appears in French medieval book illustrations in the eleventh and twelfth centuries, but is most familiar as a stone carving on medieval churches in the UK from the twelfth to sixteenth centuries (and often mistaken for a gargoyle). Many were carved during the eleventh and twelfth centuries when, during a surge in ecclesiastical building, new churches and monasteries were constructed and cathedrals were rebuilt. These were richly decorated with carvings, including representations of the Green Man himself.

The Green Man has many different guises: greenery can emerge from his mouth alone (a 'disgorging' head), or from his eyes and nose as well (a 'bloodsucker' head). Sometimes his entire face is composed of leaves (a 'foliate' head), and in some depictions oak leaves sprout from his head or grapes tumble from between his teeth.

There are many interpretations of what the Green Man represents, including an embodiment of the spirit of the forest, a mythological archetype representing the spirit of nature, and a folkloric character representing the agricultural cycle of the year. His association with forgotten traditions and nature worship has led to a revival of interest in him in recent years and he has become a symbol of ecological concerns who prompts us to once again look at our connection with nature. Festivals like the Clun Green Man Festival in

Shropshire, and Jack in the Green in Hastings, East Sussex, on May Day, celebrate the connection between his virility and the arrival of spring, and parade him as a symbol of rebirth and regeneration.

Sheela-na-gigs

During the age of medieval pilgrimage, when great numbers of people headed on foot to Rome and Santiago, churches were important way stations. Stopping to pray in a church was an integral part of the pilgrimage and stone carvings in and around churches were important ways to signal their messages to foot travellers. One of the messages that preoccupied medieval clerics was the danger of the sin of lust. Carvings, which we might now consider vulgar, of male and female genitalia were widespread, and foremost among these was a female figure with spread legs and an enlarged vulva, the sheela-na-gig.

Dating from the middle of the tenth to the middle of the twelfth centuries, there are examples of the sheela-na-gig throughout Britain and Europe, but most especially in Ireland. Pilgrimage to the shrine of St James in Spain and to Rome was commonplace there, and the word 'sheela-na-gig' derives from the Irish language. Its meaning is uncertain, but the most likely interpretations are *Sighle na gCioch* meaning 'the old hag of the breasts', or *Sile-ina-Giob* meaning 'sheela (a name for an old woman) on her hankers'. The carving has also been called The Devil Stone, the Idol, the Evil Eye Stone, Julia the Giddy, Sheila O'Dwyer, the Whore, the Witch, and the Hag of the Castle.

Many sheela-na-gigs were destroyed or vandalised in subsequent centuries when they were considered figures of embarrassment and shame. Parish priests in the seventeenth century were asked to hide them away or bury them. In more recent times their meaning and function has been perceived differently. Rather than grotesque figures of fear, representing a negative view of female sexuality, they are seen now as symbols of the power of women, sex and childbirth.

Chalk hill figures in Britain

A car journey through southern Britain, especially through Wiltshire and Devon, may well take you past the white outline of a horse or a giant looming large on a hill. Most of us remark with surprise and delight at the sight and drive on. It's much better, however, to park up and walk towards one of these figures to really make their acquaintance, or to incorporate a walk to see one as a part of a longer pilgrimage that includes other sacred sites or points of interest.

Chalk figures (known as 'geoglyphs' – literally 'land carvings') are made by scraping the vegetation and topsoil from the surface of the land until the chalk beneath is revealed. Most of those in the UK are found in the chalkland zone that runs across southern Britain from Dorset to East Anglia. There were once many more, but they have vanished through neglect – a chalk figure needs cleaning every couple of years. The ones that have lasted longest have been 'trenched', a process whereby a deeper trough is cut into the chalk in the shape of the figure and then filled with chalk rubble or rocks. This was how the White Horse of Uffington, see overleaf, was created.

Traditionally villagers would gather every year or so to renew the outline and throw a party while they were at it: dancing, singing and general carrying on were combined with the cleaning. These days several are owned by the National Trust who have taken over the duty of care. There are several notable British chalk figures.

The Cerne Abbas Giant, Dorset This massive, naked male figure is outlined with two-foot wide ditches and dominates a hillside near the village of Cerne Abbas. His 9-m-long erect phallus is his most noticeable feature and suggests that he was carved as a fertility symbol (on May Day, it points directly towards the rising sun). He holds a knobbly, oak-leaf-shaped club in his right hand and it is thought that a lion skin was once draped over his left. This has led to speculation that he could represent Hercules, who is often seen with both items in Celtic and Roman statues. On the hill above the giant is a rect-angular earthwork called the Trendle where the Wessex Morris Men still dance at sunrise on May Day, watched by hundreds of people. Throughout the history of the giant, young women and couples hoping for a child have visited him in the hope that he will bestow one upon them.

The Uffington White Horse, Oxfordshire Like an abstract sketch drawn on the hillside, this, the oldest of the UK's chalk horses, is also the most beautiful. Best seen from above (prompt-ing speculation that it was meant for the eyes of the gods), it has cantered over the rolling downland in the Ridgeway escarpment for around 3000 years. Its condition implies that it has been visited and cared for by 150 generations of people who have cleared grass and vegetation from its outline to keep it crisp and readable. (It is now managed by the National Trust.) Part of an ancient landscape that includes a Neolithic chambered tomb (Wayland's Smithy), a hill with an artificial flat top (Dragon's hill) and a hillfort, the white horse (or is it a dragon?) has been visited by pilgrims for centuries. No doubt its particular resonance and energy will continue to attract people for centuries to come.

The Long Man of Wilmington, Sussex Younger than the Cerne Abbas giant, the Long Man is no less mysterious. Cut into Windover Hill on the South Downs, he was originally thought to be an Iron-Age creation, but it's more likely that the figure was cut in the sixteenth or seventeenth century (and recarved in the nineteenth century). Slightly taller than the giant (72m compared to the giant's 55m), he is a static figure without facial features or a phallus but is accompanied by two poles, one on each side. There are various theories about what these represent: one could be a rake, the other a scythe; they could be two pilgrim's staves or two spears; or a gateway – to Heaven or the Otherworld, perhaps.

South American chalk giants

Atacama Giant The UK isn't the only country to boast chalk giants. In the Atacama desert, Chile, the figure, at 119m long, is the largest in the world. One of nearly 5000 geoglyphs (the others are much smaller) drawn on to the Cerro Unitas hill-side, it is thought he was created between AD 1000 and 1400, possibly by the Incas, although this is speculation. The parallel straight lines running from either side and from the top of his head could have had a practical purpose, maybe to align with the moon and track the time of year.

Nazca Lines In Peru a spectacular series of large and complex ancient geoglyphs of animals, birds, human figures, trees and flowers have puzzled archaeologists and anthropologists since they were discovered in 1927. Drawn by removing pebbles on the surface to reveal whitish ground beneath, they are only visible from surrounding hillsides or from the air, and were first spotted by Peruvian pilots. The figures have a geometric simplicity, with the most memorable being a hummingbird, a spider and a monkey.

Religious deities

Although mostly incorporated into a temple or other sacred building, massive statues of deities are also frequently erected as stand-alone sculptures. A focus for prayer and devotion, pilgrims head out to see them from all over the world.

Statues of the Buddha Known as Buddharūpa in Sanskrit (literally, 'the Awakened One'), Buddha statues adorn temples, hillsides and city centres, and overlook rivers. They share certain characteristics: Buddha wears a monastic robe, has elongated earlobes and a cranial bump to indicate his spirituality and awakening. The statues start to appear from the first century AD in North India, then spread to the rest of Asia, including Sri Lanka, Java and Cambodia. As Buddhism has spread, they are seen increasingly in Western countries.

Some of the most notable include the largest one in the world – the Giant Buddha of Leshan, Sichuan, Western China, a monumental figure carved from a sandstone cliff face overlooking the Dadu river; the Great Buddha of Kamakura, Japan, a bronze figure who sits in a meditative pose outside a temple; and the largest reclining Buddha in the world, the Monywa Buddha, Myanmar, which is hollow, allowing visitors to walk the length of his body from head to foot.

Hinduism This faith's many different deities are represented in three dimensions as a prompt for devotion and prayer. The statue of Vishnu in Angkor Wat, Cambodia, has six arms indicating his non-human status and is carved from a single piece of stone. He is draped with colourful clothing and pilgrims leave offerings at his feet. The Adiyogi Shiva statue in Coimbatore, Tamil Nadu, India, is a 34-m-high head and shoulders representation of the deity that was inaugurated in 2017 and stands outside the Isha Yoga complex. ('Adiyogi' means 'the first yogi' as Shiva is considered the originator of yoga.) Statues and shrines for the elephant-headed god of fortune and success, Ganesha, can be found all over Thailand (where he is called Phra Pikanet). Many are highly coloured, sumptuously decorated and enormous in scale. The largest – a reclining figure – is in Nakhon Nayok province.

Christ the Redeemer One of the most iconic religious statues, this figure stands with arms outstretched in an attitude of peace and forgiveness on the peak of the Corcovado mountain, looking down on Rio de Janeiro. Designed by French sculptor Paul Landowski, it was finished in 1931. Pilgrims climb the mountain to reach the base of the statue, but it can be seen from miles away and is a constant presence in the city. The largest Christ figure, however, is Christ the King in Świebodzin, Poland, which is 33-m tall – 3m higher that Christ the Redeemer, not that size should matter. He also has outstretched arms and flowing robes, but is topped by a gold crown.

A mindful pilgrimage to an icon or idol

- Before you set off, picture the figure in your mind. You have probably seen a photograph or a drawing, so you know what the icon looks like in two dimensions. It may look, or feel, different in three. Anticipate this.
- What is your intention? Do you want to ask the figure a question, or to seek some guidance? Do you want to thank it for something good that has happened and which it represents? Or maybe you are just curious about what it looks like. All are equally valid reasons for your pilgrimage.
- As you walk towards it – this could be a long pilgrimage across several miles, or a short walk through a church, temple or another building – think about what that figure represents. Is it a goddess, or a fertility symbol, or a figure that links you with the ancestors? If so, what does that mean to you?

- When you arrive, introduce yourself (in your head or out loud) and allow the figure to speak to you.
- Look closely at it and notice if it varies from your preconceptions. Does it have greater presence or is it less substantial than you imagined? What sort of texture is its surface, and what colour? Notice all the details. Really study it.
- If you feel it's appropriate, take a photograph to remember it. Alternatively, sketch it in a notebook or write a few thoughts on what the pilgrimage has meant to you.
- Thank the figure for the time you have spent together and say goodbye. Walk away quietly and reflect on the experience.

8

Temples

. . . the places God inhabited on Earth, the spaces where you came to make contact with the divine.

It was during one wet September in Ireland that I realised that stone circles were more than just a scenic place to stop and take a photograph on a country walk. I was on a tour of Sacred Ireland led by Peter Vallance of the Findhorn Foundation. Five of us were travelling around Ireland in a minibus, stopping at magical lakes (Lough Gur), climbing up to a burial chamber to witness the sun rise (Loughcrew cairns), and communing with spirits and legends (the Hill of Tara).

The others in the group had experienced a number of mystical experiences bordering on visions, but I had remained spiritually unmoved. I appreciated the beauty of each location, but nothing otherworldly had gone on. Not that this worried me too much – seeing these ancient and mystical places was enough, and I was cheered by Peter's advice to 'be wary of false visions'.

Towards the end of the tour, we headed south to the Beara Peninsula along twisting roads bordered with hedges of vermillion-flowered fuchsia to find Ardgroom stone circle. Peter parked up in a lay-by. We would have to walk to this one, he said, and it would be good if we did so in silence. We clambered out of the bus and, resisting the urge to chatter, began to walk in single file through a forest recently soaked with rain. The only sounds were the squelch of our footsteps, the drip of water from leaves and the flutter of birds disturbed by our movements. Shafts of sunlight broke through the forest canopy and warm earthy smells rose from the forest floor.

Pretty soon we were out on open heathland surrounded by sheep – the circle is situated on a working farm – our boots sinking into bog and mud. The first sight of a stone circle or megalith or any ancient monument is always exciting. 'There it is!' you want to shout, 'Right there!'

The Ardgroom circle was situated, as many Neolithic circles are, in a spectacular setting. The small group of stones overlooked softly rippling hills, the ocean, and, on the other side of a bay, pastel-coloured mountains. We walked around the circle and entered. Peter suggested we find a stone that spoke to us and sit down beside it. I found mine quite quickly – a triangular stone with a flat surface, ideal for resting my back against. After a moment or two, as we all settled by our stones, silence returned. It wasn't total silence, of course – the wind whispered and the sheep bleated, but all noises were gentle and unobtrusive.

This was when I began to understand the power of these places. Gradually and easily, I slipped into a state of deep peace and calm. It felt a little like being drugged or hypnotised, but without any of the unpleasant associations. I didn't have any visions and no supernatural being contacted me, but it was a profound experience – so much so that Peter had to shake me to come out of it.

The feeling of stillness, safety and calm stayed with me for days, even as the minibus lurched around corners on the way to our next destination. I can still remember how it felt sitting beside the stone. That circle on a hillside in Ireland is a place I return to in my imagination when I want to summon up a little of its serenity and security – when I want to connect with something beyond myself, something intangible but important. Like many temples, whatever their shape, age or construction, the place feels like a sanctuary and a place of profound and unknowable spirituality.

Welcome to the house of God

Imagine what it must have been like for medieval pilgrims to finally arrive at a cathedral after weeks, possibly months, of walking towards it. They would have left behind modest homes and a rustic way of living to arrive footsore, filthy and exhausted at the great cathedral doors. That first sight of a cathedral such as Durham, or Amiens in France, rising before them, splendid with pinnacles and towers and embellished with marvellous carvings and panels of glittering glass, must have been like a vision of heaven. As they walked into the unimaginably vast space with its vaulted ceilings, rose windows and soaring columns, they must surely have been struck with awe. This was exactly what the clergy, working with architects, stone masons and stained glass makers intended. Cathedrals were built to replicate an idea of heaven. They were the places God inhabited on Earth, the spaces where you came to make contact with the divine.

Making a pilgrimage to get next to God is fundamental to all religions, a tradition that has existed as long as man has. Neolithic people in Britain travelled great distances to stone temples such as Stonehenge and Avebury to attend rituals at significant times of the year. They also invested huge amounts of time and energy in constructing these complex structures, whose only purpose was to gather people together to connect with the Otherworld – whether that was a god, a spirit, or the sun and moon.

We are still drawn to these numinous prehistoric temples, which are imbued with a quality and atmosphere that suggests some element of the divine is still present. Increasing numbers of people gather at stone circles, from Stonehenge to Callanish on the Outer Hebrides, at the solstices and other Celtic festivals to greet the sunrise. The longing for a deeper spiritual meaning or a connection with the natural cycle of life makes people leave their homes and make the journey.

Christians, Buddhists, Hindus, Jews and Muslims all build temples to create a space where people can gather to communicate with the divine. Many were erected on a site that was already sacred – over a holy well, for example, or built to resemble a sacred mountain – or are plumbed into alignments with the sun and moon. Temple construction often involves sacred geometry, such as the mighty mandala made three dimensional that is the Buddhist temple of Borobudur in Indonesia, or the pyramid tombs of the pharaohs in Egypt, as well as elaborate stone carving, gilding, mosaics and complex architecture. When it comes to honouring and housing God, nothing was too grand or too complex.

As well as recreating a heaven on earth – a fitting place for God to dwell – temples are places to house magical, sacred relics, whether they relate to Buddha, a Christian saint or another holy person, for pilgrims to venerate. They are archives of the sacred where the faithful can come to pray, give thanks, leave offerings and be inspired by the lives of holy men and women.

The divine, however you envisage it, does not solely inhabit built structures, of course. Natural places are also numinous: waterfalls, ancient trees, rocky outcrops, lakes, mountains and forests are all temples, in a sense, and can provide an equally valid and less showy way of interacting with the heavenly realm.

A cathedral made of trees

The naves of Gothic cathedrals, especially those of the Perpendicular period with their tall, thin columns and fan vaults arching overhead, resemble trees in a forest. Some, including, famously, Wells Cathedral, also sprout carvings of leaves on capitals. ▶

One man, Edmund Blyth, ran with this idea and planted a cathedral out of living trees, and the result is as though one of these medieval buildings has come to arboreal life. Blyth created the tree cathedral on a 9.5-acre plot in Whipsnade, Bedfordshire as a memorial to two friends who died in the First World War. Following the cruciform floorplan of medieval cathedrals, planting began in 1930 using different tree species: lime was used for the nave, horse chestnut for the transepts. The leafy cathedral was presented to the National Trust in 1960 so anyone can enjoy a stroll under its branches. The ancient trackway the Icknield Way passes close by, making the tree cathedral a good stopping off point for pilgrims travelling along that path.

Pilgrimages to temples

Neolithic temples

Stonehenge, Wiltshire, England Every year at the summer solstice, a motley group of druids, sun worshippers, neopagans and the curious gather at the monumental stone circle Stonehenge to watch the sun come up. Clustered in the centre of the great ring, the assembled throng cheers as the sun rises over a solitary large stone about 76m away by the side of the main road. The alignment of this rough block of stone – known as the Heel Stone – with the sun and the centre of the circle, is considered proof that the ancient people who constructed

Stonehenge were sophisticated engineers and astronomers. During the winter solstice, the sun sets between three stones known as the Trilithon, making the circle of the year complete.

The magnificence of the megaliths and their astronomical alignments have drawn pilgrims to Stonehenge since it was constructed. Comprising two concentric circles of eighty blue-grey stones contained within a larger circle of 5-m-high sandstone uprights connected by lintels, it was erected in two phases dating from 2100 BC to 1100 BC. The meaning and purpose of this mighty monument has always been open to conjecture. The general consensus is that it had a religious purpose and was probably also astronomical. More fanciful theories suggest it was the work of the wizard Merlin, the relics of a Druid temple, or a UFO landing strip.

The solstices are the only time of year when there is free access to the stones: the rest of the time the nearest visitors get is about 10m away from behind a low barrier. As a pilgrimage destination it is worthwhile, though busy. There are other smaller, less-known Neolithic sites that might offer more in terms of peace and spiritual connection.

Avebury, Wiltshire, England The stones of Avebury could startle you if you weren't expecting them. Walk into the village along the road and they begin to appear in hedgerows, in fields, outside the pub, as part of the wall outside a house. They are everywhere. This is because the village has been built right at the heart of a sacred Neolithic complex. At its centre is one of the largest henges in the UK and its three stone circles. The Neolithic pilgrim would travel here from the starting place at a Sanctuary on a hill (now destroyed but marked with wooden posts), following a 2.3-km procession way of about a hundred stones (West Kennet Avenue), and passing an artificial mound (Silbury Hill, see page 65) and a chambered long barrow (West Kennet).

The reasons behind the construction of this man-made landscape are speculative, but the chances are that it was an important spiritual site. Situated virtually at the centre of southern England, it sits on the midpoint of a line drawn from the east coast to the western tip of Land's End (known as the St Michael's Line – see page 25). The Ridgeway, an ancient track considered to be Britain's oldest road and now a National Trail, passes alongside. It was positioned in a powerful place at the heart of England's prehistoric world.

Despite the addition of houses and a pub, Avebury still resonates today and is a worthy place for the modern pilgrim to head. Unlike at Stonehenge, you are free to wander where you choose. There are so many stones and deep ditches that it can take a while to get your bearings. It's the stones that make the biggest impact initially: bulky, pitted and roughly shaped, they make their presence felt. (Unfortunately, many were broken up in the eighteenth century and the splintered fragments used in house building.) Find a plan of the site and you'll realise that they are arranged in two circles side by side, contained by a large third circle of about a hundred stones. Once familiar with the stones, extend your pilgrimage to the other sites for a truly immersive insight into the spiritual world of Neolithic man.

Callanish (Calanais) Standing Stones, Isle of Lewis, Outer Hebrides, Scotland Getting to Callanish takes a bit of doing. The ferry from Ullapool, on the Scottish mainland, to Stornaway, on the Isle of Lewis, takes almost three hours. Then it's almost 20km across wild and open landscape to reach the stones. You have to really want to go there, but, like most things that take a bit of application, the rewards are worth the effort.

Seen from a distance, the tall, thin cluster of stones looks like a huddle of people gathered for a ceremony or about to participate in a dance. (Local legend has it that they are giants who were turned to stone by St Kiaran after they rejected the Christian faith.) The approach to the central circle of thirteen monoliths is along an 82-m-long avenue of guardian stones (only nine remain). At the heart of the circle is a chambered cairn in the form of a cross, and next to it is the tallest stone (about 5m high). Seen from above, the site looks like a Celtic cross. It feels like a place of great solemnity and importance.

Callanish dates from around 3400 BC and it is safe to assume that it has been a pilgrimage site ever since. The solstices continue to draw those looking to connect with the stones, the landscape and the celestial spheres – the site was probably conceived as a lunar temple or calendar. Research by archaeologist Margaret Curtis indicates that the placement of the stones was probably intended to mark the interaction between the moon and the surrounding landscape. The moon returns to the same point once every 18.6 years and Callanish plots its slow progress toward this 'lunar standstill'. At this time, the moon is so low that, once it has risen from the Pairc Hills (which resemble a woman lying on her back and are known as the Sleeping Beauty or Old Woman of the Moors), it appears to crawl along the horizon before vanishing. Observed from the end of the avenue, it sets within the tall stones of the central circle. A mighty temple if ever there was one.

Orkney, Scotland Like Avebury, Orkney off the north coast of Scotland is not about a single stone circle or lone long barrow, it's about an entire landscape. Orkney is an archipelago, but most of the important prehistoric sites are on the mainland. In this treeless, flat and remote (and also very beautiful) place, the Stones of Stenness stand in stark relief. Considered the epicentre of Neolithic Orkney, the circle of twelve stones are strikingly thin, with sharply angled tops (said to mirror the Hills of Hoy on the horizon). A walk across a narrow isthmus between two lochs will take you to the Ring of Brodgar, a wide and open circle of twenty-seven standing stones (there were sixty originally) that feels as though it's the top of the world. Between the two, archaeologists are in the process of excavating a new site – the Ness of Brodgar – which includes a massive ceremonial hall and many other structures. It appears it was an integral part of this huge ceremonial complex.

The arrival of cruise ships and coach parties mean that at certain times of the day the Ring of Brodgar and the Stones of Stenness get very busy. The modern pilgrim should head there early in the morning or at dusk – when the stones are said to come alive – for a chance to appreciate the special atmosphere and stillness of both places.

Carnac, Brittany, France Europe's largest concentration of megaliths lies scattered over three fields in northern France. About 3000 standing stones are ranged in dense rows, groups of several stones and single menhirs. The majority are organised into eleven converging rows that stretch for about 1 kilometre, with the remains of a stone circle at either end. These are positioned at regular intervals, giving the site the appearance of a knobbly cemetery or a gathering of fossilised dwarves. None of the stones is very tall: the highest is 4 metres and they reduce gradually in size along the row to about half a metre. As is usually the case with prehistoric sites, theories abound about the stones' purpose – from a place of assembly to ceremonial paths for funeral processions to an astronomical observatory. The scale of the site and its mysteriousness make it a fine destination for a pilgrimage. Plus, there's a sandy beach nearby for a post-pilgrimage plunge in the ocean.

Later temples

Angkor, Cambodia Buried in the jungle for hundreds of years, its beautiful temples, galleries and terraces strangled by creepers and the roots of banyan trees, Angkor is the world's largest religious complex. Built in the twelfth century under the rule of the King of the Khmer, Suryavarman II, and added to by successive leaders, it fell into ruin in 1431 after Angkor was sacked by Thai armies. It remained lost to the world until 1860, when French naturalist Henri Mouhot travelled there and uncovered its treasures.

What splendours he found: originally built between 1113 and 1115 as a Hindu temple dedicated to the god Vishnu, it was intended as an architectural representation of the mythical Hindu Mount Meru, which was circled by six mountain ranges with seven oceans. Spreading over 100 sq m, the complex incorporated moats, canals (some populated by crocodiles) and giant temples symbolising the holy mountain. At its centre is Angkor Wat, the most splendid, and most-visited, temple rising in tiers from terraces adorned with pavilions and galleries and capped with five ornate towers, the tallest of which is 65m high. Nearby are other grand and ornate buildings adorned with carved stone reliefs and gigantic sculptural faces of the Buddha (the temple switched to Buddhism during the reign of the last Khmer king). Entrances face west to ensure alignment with the sun on equinox and solstice days, and twenty-two designated places in Angkor Wat were used to observe the sun and the moon, creating a truly cosmic temple.

El Castillo, Chichén Itzá, Yucatan, Mexico The Mayans were a mysterious people who built sophisticated cities in the jungle of Central America, including temples constructed using complex mathematics. Yet their civilisation ended abruptly around AD 800, leaving many buildings unfinished.

One temple of many that were completed is El Castillo, built in honour of the feathered serpent god Kukulcan (also known as Quetzalcoatl). This step pyramid is a typical Mayan design: staircases ascend to a flat platform where a god – in this case Kukulcan – was honoured. What is especially remarkable about this temple is that it is a physical manifestation of the Mayan calendar. Each of the pyramid's four sides has ninety-one steps, which, multiplied and added to the top platform, come to 365 (the number of days in the year), and on each façade are fifty-two flat panels, reminders of the fifty-two years in the Mayan calendar. The temple is adorned with sculptures of the feathered serpent god, and on spring and autumn equinoxes the afternoon sun strikes the building in such a way that its shadows resemble a serpent crawling down the face of the pyramid.

Like all Mayan sites, El Castillo (which was used by the conquering Spanish as a lookout in the fifteenth century and named accordingly) is a popular visitor attraction, so expect crowds – especially when the shadowy serpent does its crawling down the pyramid thing.

Borobudur, Java, Indonesia Borobudur translates as 'the Buddhist temple on the mountain' and its resemblance to a sacred mountain is not accidental. Rising from lush, green vegetation, it is a sacred site that has been an object of pilgrimage since it was built in AD 800, and it still attracts thousands of pilgrims every year.

The floorplan of this Buddhist temple is based on the mandala, an expression of sacred geometry and a representation of the universe. It lends the building a harmonious symmetry that is entirely fitting for such a holy place. On a square base, which is orientated towards the cardinal directions, are five square levels. Above these are three upper, circular levels dotted with little stupas (dome-shaped shrines), which surround the central larger stupa, and inside the stupas are Buddha statues. Four staircases ascend from the ground to the top, and the lower levels are decorated with carved stone relief.

The Pantheon, Rome, Italy Entering the cool and beautifully proportioned Pantheon, leaving behind the bustle of the centre of Rome, can prompt a gentle exhalation of breath. Gaze up at its dome through the opening to the sky and you'll experience a little of why it was built by the Romans: it feels as though you are connected to the gods. 'Pantheon' means a collection of gods and this temple was built to honour them. Completed under the rule of the emperor Hadrian in AD 126, it is in remarkably good condition considering it is over 2000 years old. This has been attributed to its being in constant use: first by the Romans and subsequently by Christians, who dedicated it to Mary and the Martyrs. The dome is made from a lightweight form of concrete and is still the largest unreinforced dome of its type in the world. It is a miraculous building, entering it feels like going into a celestial sphere – the opening (called the oculus) draws the eye upwards toward the heavens. When Michelangelo saw it, he said it looked like the work of angels not humans. It is timeless and elemental and is well worth a pilgrimage through the hot and crowded Roman streets to find.

Durham Cathedral, Durham, England The handsome Norman cathedral that dominates this northern English town does not just house the shrine of St Cuthbert, it was built as his shrine. In the Middle Ages, and especially around 1000 to 1200, relics of saints were venerated by European Christians. The physical remains of a saint – a finger, say, or head, or even an entire body – were housed in churches, and became the focus of pilgrimage routes. Churches were built to accommodate large numbers of pilgrims who had made the journey to see them, with wider side aisles and numerous chapels to display relics.

Along with the head of St Oswald and the Lindisfarne

Gospels, St Cuthbert's body was brought to Durham by the monks of Holy Island, Lindisfarne, who fled from the Vikings in 875. They built a church to house St Cuthbert's remains. This original structure was replaced with a larger, grander building in 1093 – it is a rare example of a virtually intact Norman building and boasts a spectacular vaulted ceiling. The Shrine of St Cuthbert became an important place of pilgrimage, attracting travellers from all over Europe. His tomb remains in the east end of the cathedral and is still visited by those who come to ask him for help or to seek inspiration from his simple and holy life.

Basilica of Saint Francis, Assisi, Italy You can imagine the awe of medieval Christian pilgrims as they approached the Basilica of St Francis. Built on a hill, its massive size dominated the landscape, and still does. The pilgrims – walking to the basilica to worship the remains of St Francis, which lay in a stone tomb in the crypt – would have seen it for miles before they arrived at its door. Inside there were more wonders: frescoes by important artists such as Giotto and Cimabue lined the walls and told the story of this saintliest of saints. The grandeur and scale of the basilica, with its two churches and friary, feel at odds with the life of St Francis, who lived simply and with compassion, dedicating his life to caring for the poor and looking after animals. These days it is firmly placed on the tourist trail, with as many pilgrims coming to see the frescoes as the tomb of the saint, but it is still one of the most important places for Italy's Catholic population to go on pilgrimage.

Churches and chapels

Not all temples are spectacular in scale or embellished with carvings and rose windows. It's easy to ignore the smaller holy places, but they also offer a spiritual experience – just on a more modest scale. Ancient Christian chapels, like St Peter-on-the-Wall on the Dengie Peninsula, Essex, or the Norman St Aldhelm's Chapel on St Aldhelm's Head in Dorset, are situated on beautiful, isolated spots and have a quiet, holy presence. The fourteen churches of Romney Marsh in Kent once served a thriving community, but now stand isolated with some, such as St Thomas Becket Church in Fairfield, only accessible by foot. A day spent walking between the churches, soaking up their atmosphere and the peculiar atmosphere of the marsh itself, makes a satisfying and fascinating pilgrimage. Similarly, a walk along any pilgrimage route will pass numerous churches, many of which are worth stopping at for a breather, to sit in contemplation and to light a candle.

A mindful pilgrimage to a temple

Many of the world's greatest temples, like the Kaaba in Mecca or the Cathedral of St James in Santiago, can be reached by following long, traditional and sometimes well-organised routes. Others, like the temples at Angkor in Cambodia or the Mayan pyramids in Central America, have become tourist attractions and draw great numbers of people more interested in snaps for social media than any spiritual benefit.

Wherever possible, then, try and make your own way to the temple of your choice, and approach it quietly and with respect. Entering a sacred place surrounded by noisy chatter and ice cream scoffers can be counterproductive. Temples are powerhouses of spirituality, and pilgrims need to visit them with care – they are not places for casual, slapdash jaunts. A pilgrimage to a less-visited temple – a stone circle on a remote Cornish hill, perhaps, or a rocky tor on Dartmoor – is a different affair. These ancient places are often hidden away and need seeking out.

Before you start, consider what day you intend to make your pilgrimage. If you are going to a Neolithic site, you might like to visit when the moon is full, or at dawn on the summer solstice, or on an equinox. If it is a religious temple, it could be appropriate to go on a particular day that is important to that faith. And think about the time of day you want to arrive. Stone circles feel like they have greater magical wisdom early in the morning when they are wreathed with mist or waking up in the still light, and at dusk as darkness falls, when they become mysterious and shrouded with shadow. Then consider why you are visiting that particular sacred site. What drew you to it? What is your intention? Is there anything you want to learn or discover – about it or about yourself?

Set off and walk mindfully towards your destination, either alone or with a group of like-minded folk walking beside you in sympathetic silence. That way you notice details along the way – mushrooms springing up beside the path, clouds scudding crazily overhead, sheep noisily munching grass, the tiny petals of a wild flower. These are all part of the magical experience.

Approach the temple like this and it will take on greater significance and your pilgrimage will have a deeper meaning.

And when you get there ...

- Don't rush in. Introduce yourself and thank the temple for allowing you to enter. You don't need to say this aloud. A bow of the head or hands held in prayer for a second or two will do it.
- Harness the power of the pilgrim's favourite route: circumambulation. Walk slowly around the temple in a clockwise direction. Stone circles lend themselves to this easily and powerfully, but it works with churches and other built structures, too.
- If you are with other people, gather together for a while to focus your intention. Some might like to say a few words or recite a poem.
- Find the entrance. This will be obvious in most religious buildings but in ancient sites, it is less so. All henges and stone circles have a gap that is the correct way in. Stone circles usually have a pair of portal stones, which are larger than the others and easy to spot.
- Enter the temple and let your instinct lead you. There may be a place that draws you – a particular stone perhaps, or a quiet spot – if so, spend some time there. This would be a good place to sit and meditate and connect with your purpose and with the spirit of the place.

- Some groups participate in ritual inside the temple. This could be as simple as standing in a circle and sending light out to the cardinal points (north, south, east, west) of the earth, or more complicated – mass, purification rituals, chanting, dance and prayer. If you are in a church or cathedral, you might want to light a candle and think about someone special or attend a service. You don't have to do anything, though. As always, sitting quietly and tuning in may well be enough.
- Think about what you will take back. Not souvenirs necessarily, although those can be useful, but some part of that holy place to carry in your heart and remember how it affected you.
- Express your gratitude to the temple and leave the same way you entered – calmly and with consideration.

9

In the City

A walk in a city presents an opportunity to observe other people and to make small and exciting discoveries. As the city begins to reveal itself, the walk becomes a pilgrimage.

When you work in a city office, although you are surrounded by fascinating history, cultural attractions and splendid buildings, you might only leave your desk to make the occasional foray to the sandwich or coffee shop – or to scuttle to and from the underground station or bus stop. I've worked in a city (London) in a variety of offices and locations for most of my career, so I know this to be true.

Every so often, though, I make an effort. I decide to use my one-hour lunch break to good effect and go for a walk. Sometimes this can be an aimless meander: a saunter through the streets letting my nose guide me down alleyways, across bridges or towards a genial park café. At other times, I am more purposeful. I have something in mind that I want to see – something that draws me for whatever reason and I set out to find it. I go on a lunchtime pilgrimage.

One of my most memorable urban pilgrimages was when I worked in Clerkenwell. This area of central London, part of the borough of Islington, is a tangle of streets and public spaces with a venerable history that encompasses monastic orders, disorderly drinking dens, notorious prisons, brothels, Smithfield meat market and smart Regency terraces. In recent times it has become a fashionable destination, complete with requisite coffee shops, restaurants and architectural practices.

Curious to learn a little more about its history, I had dropped into the nearby library where, in the local history section, I learnt that the area is named after the Clerks' Well. This well, which was where clergymen (or 'clerks') performed mystery plays in the twelfth century, had been relocated, abandoned and then rediscovered in 1924 during building work on Farringdon Lane. Farringdon Lane was in walking distance of my office within the restrictions of a lunch break, so a pilgrimage to find the Clerks' Well beckoned.

I have a fascination for holy wells and seek them out on OS maps whenever I go walking in the country. I hadn't been aware, however, that I could find one in the heart of London, never mind one within walking distance of my office. So, one crisp autumn day at 1pm exactly, I persuaded my colleague Jackie to join me and stepped out of the building. Our destination wasn't very far, across a park filled with office workers eating sandwiches. As we walked, I thought about those twelfth-century monks dancing around the well performing their plays. The water in the well must have been revered by them, and the performance a vestige, perhaps, of some ancient ritual. I wondered if any dancing took place around it now. Jackie said she hoped not and, if there was, she wasn't doing any of it.

But when we reached the site of the well, we couldn't find it – no sound of running water or any built structure to house it. I scrutinised the smooth façade of a streamlined office block. The well must have been filled in and lost. But then Jackie grabbed my elbow and pointed at a blue ceramic plaque inserted into the wall: 'Clerks' Well'. A large sign with the words 'Well Court' was positioned above the door. The clues were all around.

We pressed our noses against a large panel of glass, peered in, and there it was. A deep hole surrounded by paving slabs. Reached by a short metal ladder, the well was boxed in by brick walls. On the wall was a panel of information about its history, which also stated that it was only possible to visit the well with prior permission from the council. No dancing around it for us, then.

It was, it must be said, a little disappointing not to be able to sit by the well and dip our fingers in its water. I was keen to know how clean it was and to fill a little bottle to take away with me. But we had found it and it was incredible to see it still there, still active, surrounded by all the trappings of the twenty-first century. It had also been an out-of-the-ordinary lunchtime walk that connected me with the previous inhabitants of Clerkenwell and made me think more deeply about the area where I spent much of my time. Plus, for an hour we had escaped office life, social media and the clamour of the working day.

A pilgrim in the city

Walking in the city is, for most of us, about getting somewhere. Whether it's to work, to pick up the children, to meet a friend, or to buy a pint of milk, the journey is seen as a necessary nuisance: something to be endured to get to where we want to be. With the amount of traffic increasing and high streets and shopping malls resembling each other more and more, this has become increasingly the case.

As a result, we tend to think of the activity of 'walking' as something to save for the weekend, for a country lane or a coastal path, which is a shame: there is much to be gained from a stroll through the city if time is taken to enjoy it and a destination kept in mind. The best option is to alternate the two, without favouring either. A walk in a city presents an opportunity to observe other people and to make small and exciting discoveries. A rural walk, on the other hand, is generally a more contemplative experience.

When we hurry through the streets, we stop paying attention to everything around us. Despite being bombarded with all manner of sensory onslaughts, from the smell of coffee to billboards, graffiti, neon lights, we keep our heads down and march on. Everyone has a different reason to be out and about and everyone is in a hurry. However, a walk through a city needn't be an obstacle course seemingly designed to thwart progress and annoy. If, instead of rushing to a destination, we walk there slowly and mindfully, and if the destination is somewhere of significance, the city becomes an entirely different place. As the city begins to reveal itself, the walk becomes a pilgrimage.

A city pilgrim becomes an active observer of places and people. Things that shoppers and commuters pass by, the pilgrim notices: an architectural detail above a shop front, ivy pushing its way through a crack in a wall, a sorrowful face in a coffee shop window. Walking slowly and steadily enables you to look around and notice. As you move forwards, the scenery constantly shifts. One minute you pass a row of Indian restaurants, the next you are walking through a market, then past a crowd of drinkers outside a pub. It can feel like walking through a film set.

You can do all of this anonymously: unlike walking through a village or along a country footpath, no one notices you in a city – everyone is too intent on their own purpose. But you can notice *them*. You become the observer.

The writer Virginia Woolf, famously an inhabitant of Bloomsbury in London, enjoyed the invisibility of walking through the city and becoming 'part of that vast republican army of anonymous trampers'. Her senses were kept on alert, looking, 'seeing life' – a process she called 'street haunting'. Viewed through her novelist's eye, the details of the city became vivid and engrossing. She included one walk (albeit a fairly short one) in her novel *Mrs Dalloway*, where Clarissa Dalloway walks through central London to pick up some flowers for a party she is hosting that evening. Clarissa, she writes, 'had the oddest sense of being herself invisible; unseen; unknown.'

This immersion in, and observation of, city life was

promoted by 'flaneurs' in nineteenth-century Paris (or 'fla-neuse' if they were female). Flaneurs sauntered through an urban landscape, led by instinct or curiosity, without a map or a purpose, making observations as they went. Its originator, the poet Charles Baudelaire described this 'gentleman stroller of city streets' and the 'immense joy' he experiences, 'to see the world, to be at the centre of the world, and yet to remain hidden from the world.'

City pilgrims have much in common with flaneurs – they too are aware of what's going on around them in all its detail, feeling invisible yet part of the crowd – but they walk with a goal in mind. This creates a route to follow and a direction in which to head. The pavements and streets walked by the modern pilgrim are well-trodden: walk along any city street and you tread in the footsteps of countless others who went that way before you. It's something to keep in mind as you step onwards, passing through the crowds, heading towards your destination.

A neighbourhood pilgrimage

You don't need to be in the centre of a big city to experience an urban pilgrimage. If you live in a town or in the suburbs, stepping out of your front door and walking through your own neighbourhood works just as well. Head for somewhere you haven't been before – a church, perhaps, or a wood – and make it the focus of your pilgrimage. As you walk, look at your sur-roundings as though you are new to the area and seeing them for the first time.

Lunchtime pilgrimages

The temptation to grab a sandwich and eat it at your desk is hard to resist: there's always work to get on with and emails to answer, and if you bring your own lunch into the office you may not get out at all. Instead of sitting dormant in front of your computer, consider a mini pilgrimage. Choose a place that you can walk to and back from within an hour, and you will return to work revived and, to be honest, a little bit smug. Unlike your co-workers who have been glued to screens and mired in monotony, you have been out and accomplished something.

Let the American poet Frank O'Hara be your inspiration. Without skipping lunch (his favourite meal), he liked to stroll around New York in his lunch hour. His observations, combined with what was going on in his life at the time, informed his poetry, which he gathered together in the book *Lunch Poems*.

Writing poetry in your lunch hour may be a stretch, but a mini pilgrimage could inspire you to be creative. You could research statues within walking distance, for example, then head off to find them. Thoughts and ideas may come to you as you walk, which can be used as material for your own creative work. There are many other possibilities.

Pilgrimages in urban surroundings

Wells Although many ancient wells in cities have vanished, many still exist and, with a bit of sleuthing, can be found gushing from sides of roads or bubbling up inside specifically constructed buildings. Districts of the city with 'well' in their name provide obvious clues (the theatre at Sadler's Well in London has incorporated the well into the fabric of the building, for example), and maps found in local history sections of libraries will point you in the right direction. Often these wells can be found near churches or churchyards, or in parks: St Margaret's Well and St Anthony's Well, both in Edinburgh, are in Holyrood Park, for example. A quick internet search will reveal others.

Churches, chapels and cathedrals Step into a church and, whether you are a believer or not, you enter a cool, quiet place that is instantly calming. Hallowed, numinous places such as these make a welcome respite from the hurly-burly of the city streets outside. They are places to sit quietly and reflect, to stop the frenetic pace of life for a moment or two. There is also much of interest to explore and admire, including the architecture, the stained glass and the tombs of the great and the good. Light a candle when you are there to distil your thoughts or to remember a loved one: it always feels powerful and focuses the mind, whatever your faith or beliefs. Easy to find and often overlooked, churches are well worth seeking out as destinations for your city pilgrimage. The bigger ones might even have relics of saints and be a traditional medieval pilgrimage church.

A word of caution: remember to be respectful if there is a service in progress.

Lost rivers During the Victorian period many of the rivers coursing through the UK's cities were used as open sewers. The smell and sanitation problems that arose resulted in these rivers being covered over and 'buried' beneath the streets. Traces of these 'lost' rivers can still be found, most notably in London. The best-known is the River Fleet, which was incorporated into a sewer system following pollution caused by butchers throwing animal carcasses into it. It now flows underground from Hampstead and Highgate Ponds in north London to Blackfriars Bridge on the River Thames. Find other hidden rivers at local museums and see if you can follow their course above ground through the city to where they finally emerge.

Landmarks To keep your pilgrimage meaningful and to avoid becoming one more snap-happy tourist, choose your city landmark carefully. Rather than see a castle, palace or gallery as yet another place to tick off on a sightseeing list, find one that resonates with you for a particular reason. This could be due to some family connection, or because its history fascinates you. Walk to it from wherever you are staying, keeping it in mind as you do so. As you approach, and it grows larger in your line of vision, it will have greater significance and the experience will be more memorable.

Blue plaques Placed by English Heritage on buildings specifically in London, these indicate where notable people once lived (see page 188). Other commemorative plaque schemes exist in cities throughout the UK and in Paris, Rome, Oslo and Dublin, among others.

Statues and monuments Most cities and large towns have statues of people who have contributed significantly to that place. Many of these are of royalty, parliamentarians or religious and military figures, but there are others, too. Artists, poets, musicians and scientists can all be found frozen in time in characteristic poses. In Wrocław, Poland, there is even a 'Monument to the Anonymous Passerby'. Most people walk past these kinds of statues hardly noticing who they are. Find one that has meaning to you, make your pilgrimage there, and reflect on that person's life and its inspiration.

Squares These pockets of traffic-free space in urban settings make a peaceful place to head on a city pilgrimage. Many are part of a larger town-planning scheme, surrounded by handsome terraces and planted with shady trees and flowering borders. Others have interesting histories: Coram's Fields in London was once the site of the Foundling Hospital established by Thomas Coram in 1739, where abandoned children were cared for. It's now a park for children to enjoy. The Place des Vosges in Paris is the oldest planned square in the city and is surrounded by trees and houses built in the Louis XIII-style of architecture, one of which houses the Victor Hugo Museum. Most cities have similarly interesting squares. They also have benches for the weary pilgrim to rest.

Parks These welcome patches of greenery attract anyone wanting a restful place to pause and step away from the city's frenetic pace. City parks are the places where local people head during their leisure hours or office workers eat their lunch. In Central Park, New York, you will find runners, strollers, sandwich eaters and yoga classes (and John Lennon's memorial 'Strawberry Fields' – a place of pilgrimage if ever there was one). Barrancas de Belgrano in Buenos Aires has a bandstand where local people dance tango. And Shinjuku Gyoen park in Tokyo turns a glorious pink in the spring when the cherry trees burst into blossom.

Psychogeography

The more urban walks you do and the more you get into it, the more likelihood that you will come across talk of 'psychogeography'. The concept was conceived by the French Marxist philosopher Guy Debord in 1955 as a way of engaging pedestrians with their environment. It encouraged them to step away from their predictable paths and explore. Loosely, it is a study of the effect of the environment, most frequently the city landscape, on the emotions and behaviour of the individual.

More recently, writer Will Self described his walks through urbanscapes in a series of columns actually called 'Psychogeography'. Before him, author and urban explorer Iain Sinclair popularised the notion in his books *Lights Out for the Territory: Nine Routes Across London* and *London Orbital: A Walk Around the M25*. As psychogeography has evolved, romantic and occult ideas such as earth mysteries and ley lines have been woven into its urban perambulations, with references to 'secret mythologies' and 'psychic landscapes': all ways of making the everyday more interesting by imbuing it with elements of the arcane.

A mindful city pilgrimage

Whether you live in a city or are visiting one, there will be plenty of opportunities to head out purposefully and explore it. This could be early on a Sunday morning before people start to stir and the streets are quiet, or a weekday lunchtime when office workers are out buying their lunch and the pavements are packed, or at dusk when the streetlights start to pierce the darkness. Whenever you choose, one thing is for certain: there will be plenty to see.

- First decide where you are heading. It should be somewhere that has meaning or significance to you. Keep the place in mind and imagine what it might be like when you reach it.
- Stand tall and feel the ground beneath your feet. Are you on the pavement? Can you feel its firm, flat surface under the soles of your shoes?
- Start walking and, as you do, notice how your body responds to different surfaces – Tarmac, concrete, grass – and what they feel like to walk on.
- It's hard to keep up a regular rhythm when walking through the city, so instead appreciate how your body responds to obstructions, shifts in direction, changes in pace.
- Be vigilant and really notice what is going on around you: the people walking nearby; the architecture; shop signs; all the minutiae of city life.

- Listen to the noises of the street and try to differentiate one from the other: traffic passing by, a child's cry, the hum of air conditioning from a shop, a dog yapping.
- Stop every so often and touch different surfaces – bark, wood, glass, stone, the fur on an animal – and compare how they feel.
- If it's a sunny day, or if you are walking at night beneath streetlights, keep an eye on your shadow and watch as it moves and interplays with other people's.

And when you get there ... Don't rush away. Does the place look and feel as you expected, or has it surprised you? Take time to get to know it. Then retrace your steps and head home.

10

Following in the Footsteps

*Walking with a person in mind, along a
route that had significance to them, is a meditative
process during which thoughts and memories arise
that are unprompted and unexpected.*

Before my father married my mother and settled down he had
a colourful, bohemian life. He wore a beard (unusual in the
1950s), read poetry (mostly to woo young women), bred pigs (he
rode one to the pub) and rocked around the country in a car
he built himself. Much of this itinerant and unconventional
lifestyle was driven by his urge to replace the confines of the
steel town in South Wales where he grew up with a more rural
and outdoors way of life, which he craved.

During one of his adventures he ended up at the religious
community led by artist Eric Gill at Capel-y-ffin, near the

English-Welsh border. Although he never told us much about what he did there or, tantilisingly, what Eric Gill was like, he always spoke of the remote hamlet and Llanthony Abbey further down the valley with reverence.

Years later, shortly after he died, I was staying in Hay-on-Wye with some friends when I realised that Capel-y-ffin was eight miles away, close enough to walk to. I decided to make a pilgrimage to the place that had meant so much to my dad, and to try to understand why it was important to him.

The path began comfortably but soon rose steeply. I had set off without paying enough attention to the map and hadn't realised that the route would take me to Gospel Pass, the highest pass in Wales. Needless to say, the walking got tough quickly and the road through the Black Mountains was endless and pretty exhausting. But I plodded on, one step at a time, each one getting me closer to my destination. At the pass, I stopped for a breather and took in the enormous views before beginning the descent.

As I strode downhill across moorland populated by sheep and ponies, into the wooded valley below, I thought of my father as a young man, fit and bearded and eager to experience life away from the steelworks, doing the same. It was a good image to replace, or at least hold alongside, my final memory of him as an old man. When I arrived at the little hamlet, tucked away in a forgotten and timeless spot, and found the monastery (then in a state of disrepair, now self-catering accommodation), I could picture him coming towards me in an artist's smock and pair of sandals, searching for a different way of living, his life stretching before him full of promise.

Footsteps of a friend

Retracing a journey on foot made by someone you loved who has died or moved away, can ease the pain of missing them a little. The physical and rhythmic act of walking helps to process the loss. It's hard to understand why – it just does. It feels like a better, more active, way to deal with grief than staying indoors, static and mournful.

This act of personal pilgrimage can take several forms. It could involve retracing a journey you made together to a place that has meaning for you: a beach where you paddled; a lay-by where you ate your sandwiches; a mountain you both clambered up. Or you could repeat a memorable trip they took without you, either before they knew you or with other people, but which they told you about. Or you could return to walk a favourite route of theirs, whether it was a coastal footpath, the daily walk to the park with the dog or something else altogether.

Whichever it is, chances are that this personal pilgrimage will be loaded with meaning and memories. These will help you feel close to that person again and rekindle things about them that you had forgotten. Walking with a person in mind, along a route that had significance to them, is a meditative process during which thoughts and memories arise that are unprompted and unexpected.

Whether the person in question is a family member, an absent lover or a missing friend, retrace their steps and they become a presence walking beside you. As you track their chosen path, or revisit one you walked together, you observe what they once observed, enjoy sights they once saw, and struggle across tricky terrain where they once struggled. As you seek to discover why they chose the route they did, and what it meant to them, a connection is built between the two of you, even though you are far apart in distance or in time.

Before you set out on your personal pilgrimage, put something that reminds you of that person in your pocket. This could be a photograph, a letter or anything small, personal and significant that you can tuck away. As you walk, take it out every so often, look at it, hold and feel it, and think about the absent person.

As you continue to walk, look around you and notice things that they would have noticed. What would have triggered their interest or amused them? Was there a view they loved or that you enjoyed together? Did they always stop and sit somewhere? Make sure you sit there, too. Did they enjoy a drink or a meal at a favourite place? Remember to pause and eat something that reminds you of them.

As you near your destination, reflect on what that person was like and what they meant to you. Consider what they brought to your life and why you are grateful that you knew them.

And when you get there ... This pilgrimage ends at a place that resonated with the person in your thoughts. It could be that river you swam in together, their childhood home that you have searched for and found, a restaurant where you shared a great meal, somewhere they talked about but which you have never visited, or the place you last saw them.

Don't rush off now you've arrived, take a few moments

to think about your absent companion and how they have enriched your life. If it feels right, write your thoughts in a notebook or simply let them surface, acknowledge them, then tuck them away in your memory.

A mindful journey in the footsteps of a travel writer

Follow the footsteps of an adventurous traveller and you will be introduced to new and exciting places. You may also feel like you begin to know them. If you're feeling adventurous, this pilgrimage could spur you on to do something similarly intrepid yourself. The adventurer may have written about their travels in a book, or another writer and/or film maker could have documented their journey. See this as a roadmap for your own pilgrimage. Who knows where it might lead?

Retracing the entire path of the more intrepid explorers, adventurers and travel writers is probably a little ambitious for most of us, but it may be possible to walk part of their journey to get a flavour of what they experienced. Once in the country they travelled through, you can pick up their trail using their experiences as your guide. This could be as modest as retracing the poet John Betjeman's potterings around English churches or, more boldly, following Robert Macfarlane along the same paths he wrote about in *The Old Ways*. Or it could be a massive adventure like following Guy Stagg, who walked a 3420-mile pilgrimage to Jerusalem. The choice is yours!

On the following pages you'll find some inspiring travel writers to follow.

Walking Home, **Simon Armitage** The Yorkshire poet became a 'modern troubadour' and walked the Pennine Way to the village where he was born, singing (reading poems, that is) for his supper along the way.

As I Walked Out One Midsummer Morning, **Laurie Lee** The evocative tale of a young man in the 1930s setting out on foot from a Cotswolds village to London and then Spain, where he is trapped by the outbreak of the Spanish Civil War.

The Old Ways: A Journey on Foot, **Robert Macfarlane** Walks following pilgrimage paths, sea roads, prehistoric tracks and ancient rights of way, guided by the spirit of poet Edward Thomas.

The Crossway, **Guy Stagg** An immense walk, mostly undertaken alone, of 3420 miles from Canterbury to Jerusalem, relying on the generosity of strangers along the way.

Walking the Woods and the Water, **Nick Hunt** Patrick Leigh Fermor set out, aged eighteen, to walk across Europe 'like a tramp, a pilgrim or a wandering scholar'. Nick Hunt follows his footsteps all the way to Istanbul.

Wild: A Journey from Lost to Found, **Cheryl Strayed** A 1100-mile solo hike along the West Coast of America, looking to make sense of things following a series of domestic calamities.

A Walk in the Woods, **Bill Bryson** The Appalachian Trail is the longest continuous footpath in the world. Bryson and a companion walked it trying to dodge bears, ticks and other hikers as they did so.

The Land Beyond, **Leon McCarron** A solo walk through the Middle East from Jerusalem along pilgrimage and trading routes to the deserts of the Sinai.

Pyschogeography, **Will Self** A series of essays about journeys taken on foot, mostly through urban landscapes, including one from his home to Heathrow, and then from JFK airport in New York to downtown Manhattan.

The Salt Path, **Raynor Winn** A moving memoir about walking the 630-mile South West Coast Path with a terminally ill husband following the loss of their home and livelihood.

Trains and Buttered Toast, **John Betjeman** Essays on a now-lost Britain that involves a lot of pottering about in small villages and seaside towns.

Before you set off, read about the traveller's journey, whether it's their own account or written by someone else. Try and understand their motivation for their walk and see if it matches your own. What destination did they have in mind and what did they hope to discover when they arrived? Are you using their trip as a template or are you searching for something yourself? Keep the book with you and, as you walk, compare your experience with theirs and see how the two match up (or don't).

And when you get there ...

- Thank the original traveller for taking you along the path and showing you the way.
- Assess what the pilgrimage has meant to you and if it resonates with what it meant to them. Has it affected your opinion of them?
- Think about how the walk will inspire you to make more pilgrimages yourself.

 Final footsteps

All of our heroes, whether they are family and friends, writers, musicians, scientists, campaigners or sportsmen, die and are buried or cremated somewhere. Seeking the location and going on a pilgrimage to pay respects is in the fine tradition of ancestor worship and keeps that person alive in your memory.

A pilgrimage to a cemetery or to a tomb can also be an opportunity to consider someone's life, what they achieved and what it meant to you. Some of the more famous graves are busy with visitors: musician Jim Morrison's tomb in Père Lachaise cemetery in Paris is festooned with flowers and messages, as is Oscar Wilde's, which is nearby. Poet Sylvia Plath's modest grave in Heptonstall, Yorkshire, although tucked away in a corner of the cemetery, is visited by many of her fans, some of whom leave pens as an offering. Other graves, whether they are in a grand cathedral, a modest country churchyard or a plaque in a crematorium, may be less popular and more challenging to find, but are well worth it, providing a quiet place to sit and reflect on that person's life and its meaning to you.

The singer and poet Patti Smith describes the pilgrimages she has made to graves of people who have had an important influence on her in a memoir *M Train*. These include the author Jean Genet in Morocco; in Japan, the film director and author Yukio Mishima, and the film director Akira Kurosawa; and Sylvia Plath in Heptonstall, whose grave she visited three times. On the last of these three visits, she 'sat quietly by the grave, conscious of a rare and suspended peace'.

She also takes Polaroid photographs of each grave she visits. She has stacks of these that she keeps and sometimes spreads out in front of her like 'an imagined celestial team'.

Where to find your hero

In a cathedral People of note are frequently buried in the larger cathedrals. They are often the final resting places of royalty and members of the clergy, who have sizeable tombs, but other well-known names can be found. Charles Dickens, Geoffrey Chaucer and Rudyard Kipling, among others, are buried in 'Poet's Corner' in the south transept of Westminster Abbey. Jane Austen is buried in Winchester Cathedral – there is also a brass plaque and a window in her memory. The artist JMW Turner and Horatio Nelson are buried in St Paul's Cathedral and William Shakespeare's grave is in Holy Trinity Church, Stratford-upon-Avon.

In a cemetery Certain cemeteries are known for a significant number of famous burials. Among those who ended up in Highgate Cemetery in London, for example, are George Eliot, Douglas Adams and Malcolm McLaren. In the Forest Lawn Memorial Park, Glendale, California, you will find memorials for Elizabeth Taylor, Bette Davis, Michael Jackson, Walt Disney and Nat King Cole.

In a churchyard As is the case with comedian and writer Spike Milligan, whose grave is in Winchelsea, East Sussex (with the epitaph 'I told you I was ill'), other well-known people are buried in the churchyard near their homes or in the city where they lived. Franz Kafka is buried in the New Jewish Cemetery in Prague, for example, and poets John Keats and Percy Bysshe Shelley are buried in the Protestant cemetery in Rome. Composers Ludwig van Beethoven, Johannes Brahms and Franz Schubert are all buried in the Zentralfriedhof Cemetery in Vienna, where there is also a memorial to Wolfgang Amadeus Mozart. To find a particular person who interests you, search findagrave.com, which locates graves worldwide.

Remembered on a blue plaque Over nine hundred notable men and women are honoured on blue plaques on London streets, many erected on the homes in which they lived. A visit to one or several that have meaning to you makes for a fascinating and respectful pilgrimage. (For a list of blue plaques, see english-heritage.org.uk/visit/blue-plaques.)

The fallen

Cities all over the world have memorials at their heart, honouring those who died during different wars in service of their country. They are poignant and solemn places to make a pilgrimage, often impressive and imaginative in scale, and with a chilling list of names of those who were lost in battle. Often used as a place to meet for a commemorative service, they become a focus for grief and remembrance.   ▶

Graves of military personnel killed during wars, especially the First and Second World Wars, and including the graves of unknown soldiers, are also visited by relatives and friends, who often travel a long way to find them.

The Commonwealth War Graves Commission maintains cemeteries and memorials at 23,000 locations in over 150 countries, commemorating those who died in the First and Second World Wars. Its website can help you trace an individual.

The Animals in War Memorial in Hyde Park, London, honours the animals who died in war and conflicts, including horses, mules and dogs. It has a small inscription: *'They had no choice'*.

A mindful journey to a final resting place

As you enter the cemetery or place of burial, walk towards your hero with them in mind. Take a copy of one of their books, a postcard of their work, or listen to a piece of their music as you approach.

And when you get there ...

- Thank them for what they have contributed to your life and to the lives of others.
- Read a passage from one of their books (not necessarily aloud), listen (on headphones) to

music they composed, or honour them in some other way that feels right.

- Sweep leaves and other debris from the gravestone as a thoughtful act.
- If appropriate, leave an offering or take a photograph.
- Think about how they have inspired you so far, and what they will encourage you to do next.

Fictional footsteps

The setting of a novel can be as memorable as the plot or the characters. If the author has done their job, the reader becomes thoroughly transported to, and immersed in, a place and a time. It can feel disorientating to finish a book and find yourself lying on the sofa at home rather than, say, in Christopher Isherwood's Berlin before the Second World War, or at a party on Long Island in the 1920s with Jay Gatsby.

A great novel takes you to that place in your imagination. Set off on a pilgrimage to the actual place and you experience it in reality. By tracing the trails laid down in a book, you may see the story differently and get a new perspective on the writer. As with all pilgrimages, a fixed mission forces you to be present rather than to meander and dawdle. Sights and sounds become vivid and have extra meaning if they are seen in the context of a favourite book. Many of them will have changed since the book was written, of course, or you may find that the writer exaggerated or invented elements of the place, but this comparison is part of the fascination and the pleasure.

Places in fiction

Newfoundland *The Shipping News* by E Annie Proulx
Dublin, Ireland *The Dubliners* by James Joyce
Edinburgh, Scotland *The Inspector Rebus* novels by Ian Rankin
Stockholm, Sweden *The Millennium Trilogy* by Stieg Larsson
London *Absolute Beginners* by Colin McInnes; *Brick Lane* by Monica Ali; *Little Dorrit* by Charles Dickens
Hollywood, California *The Day of the Locust* by Nathanael West
Paris *The Dud Avocado* by Elaine Dundy
New York *The Catcher in the Rye* by J D Salinger; *A Little Life* by Hanya Yanagihara; *The Goldfinch* by Donna Tartt
Kerala *The God of Small Things* by Arundhati Roy
Vienna *The Third Man* by Graham Greene
Berlin *I am a Camera* by Christopher Isherwood
Botswana *The No. 1 Ladies' Detective Agency* by Alexander McCall Smith

Where they wrote

What attracts so many visitors to Jane Austen's house and its museum in Hampshire is that they get to see where Jane wrote her novels, where she ate, where she slept and the garden in which she wandered. For an hour or so, the visitor has a chance to live in her world. This experience can be extended further by walking from her house through the fields and past churches where she strolled to neighbouring villages. The true Austen pilgrim could even undertake the 16-mile walk to Winchester Cathedral, where she is buried.

Other writers' homes have been carefully preserved with original pieces of furniture in place (including the all-important writer's desk) and opened as museums. They too make an edifying pilgrimage destination.

Flannery O'Connor Andalusia Farm, Milledgeville, Georgia; gcsu.edu/andalusia

Henry James and E F Benson Lamb House, Rye, East Sussex; nationaltrust.org.uk/lamb-house

Dylan Thomas Boathouse, Laugharne, Camarthenshire; dylanthomasboathouse.com

Virginia Woolf Monk's House, Rodmell, Lewes, East Sussex; nationaltrust.org.uk/monks-house

Rudyard Kipling Bateman's, Burwash, East Sussex; nationaltrust.org.uk/batemans

Jane Austen Jane Austen's House Museum, Chawton, Hampshire; jane-austens-house-museum.org.uk

William Faulkner Rowan Oak, Oxford, Massachusetts; rowanoak.com

John Milton Milton's Cottage Museum, Chalfont St Giles, Buckinghamshire; miltonscottage.org

The Brontë Sisters Brontë Parsonage Museum, Haworth, Yorkshire; bronte.org.uk

The Dymock Poets

Devotees of this literary group will find not just a single destination but an entire landscape to visit. The six poets, Robert Frost, Edward Thomas, Lascelles Abercrombie, Rupert Brooke, Wilfrid Gibson and John Drinkwater, lived in and around the village of Dymock in the valley of the River Leadon in Herefordshire between 1911 and 1914, and drew much inspiration from their surroundings. The group disbanded when Edward Thomas was killed in action in 1917 during the First World War. The Friends of the Dymock Poets have drawn up paths that follow the perambulations of the writers around this beautiful part of the world, which make fine routes for any literary pilgrim to follow. See dymockpoets.org.uk

A musical diversion

Certain songs, like books, mention places that take on a mythic, romantic quality the more they are played. Some are real and others imagined. Most have particular associations for the songwriter and are freighted with personal meaning. Subsequently, they become meaningful to us as we listen to them and add associations of our own. Seek out these places and see how the lyrics match your preconceptions. Here are a few for inspiration:

'Montague Terrace (In Blue)' Scott Walker
'59 Lyndhurst Grove' Pulp
'Denmark Street' The Kinks
'Warwick Avenue' Duffy
'On Broadway' The Drifters
'Route 66' Chuck Berry
'Penny Lane' The Beatles
'Thunder Road' Bruce Springsteen

A mindful pilgrimage to a place in a song

- Establish first if the place is real – many songwriters create imaginary landscapes or disguise real locations by inventing new names.
- Does the song have an emotional connection for you? It may have a romantic association or be a favourite song of someone you have lost. If this is the case, take time to think of that person and bring something that reminds you of them along on your pilgrimage.
- Scour web pages and maps, and learn about the history of the place. Try to understand why the songwriter chose it as a subject.
- Set off to find it. Don't forget to have a recording of the song and headphones with you so that you can play it when you get there.
- On arrival, play the song and find somewhere to sit and listen to it.
- Is the place as you imagined? What kind of

emotions has it triggered? Jot down a few thoughts in your notebook.

- Think of a street that is important to you. Can you write a song about it?

A pilgrimage for a dying friend

In 1974, the German film director Werner Herzog heard that his friend, the film historian Lotte Eisner, was critically ill. He decided to walk hundreds of miles from Munich to Paris to see her, believing that by making this pilgrimage she would recover. Herzog wrote an account of his pilgrimage in his book *Of Walking in Ice: Munich–Paris, 23 November – 14 December 1974*. 'I set off ... in full faith believing that she would stay alive if I came on foot,' he wrote. 'We would not permit her death.' His heroic and arduous walk through severe winter weather to her bedside took twenty-one days and is a testament to his faith: she recovered and lived for another ten years – an extreme and unusual route to recovery but, in this case, effective.

The Unlikely Pilgrimage of Harold Fry by Rachel Joyce is a fictional account of a similar pilgrimage, except that the pilgrim is a 65-year-old man walking from Devon to Berwick-upon-Tweed on hearing of the terminal illness of an old colleague, Queenie. As he walks, he tries to resolve issues from his past, including the death of his son and abandonment by his mother. His pilgrimage fails to keep Queenie alive but does succeed in his laying some ghosts to rest and reigniting his love for his wife.

11

Faith Routes

All over the world, faiths of all persuasions
put pilgrimage at the heart of their beliefs.
Among the many things that pilgrimage provides
are an end point, a purpose and a real
sense of achievement.

The best-known account of a pilgrimage is still Geoffrey Chaucer's *The Canterbury Tales*, which was written at the end of the fourteenth century. This collection of twenty-four stories, each told by a pilgrim from a different social class or profession as they walked to Canterbury Cathedral, is a snapshot of medieval life, but also demonstrates what pilgrimages can be like, both then and now. Gather a group of people with a common spiritual purpose – in Chaucer's pilgrims' case, to see the shrine of Thomas Becket – and you will assemble people from different backgrounds, different ages and with different tales to tell. Pilgrimage need not always be a solo activity. Walking with others is equally valid. It is an opportunity to meet people you would never normally come across, to buoy each other's spirits when the going gets tough, and to share your thoughts and stories as you walk side by side.

I thought about this one April morning as my friend Liz and I set out with Will Parsons and Guy Hayward of the British Pilgrimage Trust. With around 20 other pilgrims we were about to walk part of the Old Way, which starts at Southampton and ends at Canterbury Cathedral. Will and Guy have done much to revive pilgrimage in the UK with their winning blend of enthusiasm, knowledge, choral singing and historical detective work. Whereas Chaucer's pilgrims walked from Southwark along Watling Street to Canterbury, other medieval pilgrims followed a 120-mile route (and ancient track) from Winchester. Known as the Pilgrim's Way, it was rediscovered by writer, historian and long-distance walker Hilaire Belloc and is still walked by pilgrims today.

However, by studying the Gough Map of Great Britain, which was drawn up around 1360 and is one of the earliest maps of Britain to possess a degree of accuracy, Will and Guy came across another pilgrimage route. This path, which was clearly marked on the map, ran from Southampton to Canterbury and was sprinkled with monastic houses, ancient sites and wells. When pilgrimage was banned by Henry VIII during the Reformation, the path, like many others across the country, ceased to be walked and faded from view. Will and Guy have made it their mission to reignite interest in this forgotten path, which they call the Old Way, by taking people on pilgrimage along it and by spreading the word about it and other British pilgrimage routes through media appearances and general hearty evangelism.

This is how Liz and I came to be at Ham Street station in Kent on a sparkling spring morning, cautiously eyeing up the other pilgrims who would be our companions for the next three days. We were to walk the last section of the 217-mile Old Way that would, like Chaucer's pilgrimage, takes us to Canterbury Cathedral – the entire route takes about a fortnight. Equipped with a hazel staff each, we set off along a wooded track lined with bluebells and sprinkled with sunlight. A most promising start to our pilgrimage and the best way I can think of to spend the last days of April.

The Old Way is more rural than the Pilgrim's Way, passing through ancient flint villages and over downland to wells and woods. It crosses one major road but otherwise traffic is avoided and the route knits together other pathways, including the Solent Way, the North Downs Way and the Royal Military Canal. I'm sure it is easy to navigate, but it was a relief to hand over directions to Will and Guy – especially as there were so many pilgrims to get to know.

It can be hard to keep mindful when there is social activity going on around you (for ways to deal with this, see below). It reminded me of Nan Shepherd's reaction to walking with 'brilliant young people' in her book, *The Living Mountain*. Their 'entertaining and witty and incessant' talk left her feeling 'weary and dispirited because the hill did not speak'. For a while, the unfolding countryside was also silent as fellow pilgrims, by dint of curiosity and a series of questions, established who we were, and we did the same to them.

Our group, it turned out, was a mixture of, among others, seasoned walkers, a Sikh convert, a teacher, a theatre director, a journalist and an IT specialist. None were particularly religious, but all of us were driven by an urge to walk with a purpose and were in search of something. Eventually, the chatter petered out and Liz and I, putting our mind to the walk, left a gap between us and our nearest pilgrims and walked on quietly and companionably, in the way that good friends do.

Will and Guy know the route thoroughly so were able to guide us to the places we wouldn't have found on our own. These included churches in sleepy villages, which we walked around before entering in true pilgrimage circumambulation style, and inside which they frequently burst into song (Guy is a champion of evensong and they are both former choristers). One night was spent sleeping in a church, lying on pews in our sleeping bags – part of an initiative of theirs to encourage more churches to open their doors and provide accommodation for pilgrims. The other night we slept in the grounds of a medieval castle, where we filled bottles with water from the well while singing a medieval song: 'Water Flows, Life is Given / Rises from Earth / Falls from Heaven.' (We tipped this water into a well on arrival in Canterbury to unite the two wells and to mark an end to our pilgrimage.)

On the final day, with Canterbury seven miles away, we stopped off at a neglected well the size of a pool, where fellow pilgrims splashed about in their swimmers as Liz and I watched from the side like prim (but dry) aunts. One of the last stretches of truly rural paths took us through another bluebell wood. Will suggested that we walk in silence, and it was blissful to tread quietly and absorb our magical surroundings. Walking slowly and meditatively helped me to notice all the details along the path – from lichen-covered stumps to the curl of a bluebell petal. I can still see it now and it is one of the lasting impressions I have of the walk.

Shortly after, we stopped at the summit of a hill. In the distance, hazy in the afternoon sun, was Canterbury Cathedral, the end of our pilgrimage. Later that day we would walk into the cathedral with our staffs as evensong started, much as Chaucer's pilgrims would have done. Until then, standing on the hill with my fellow modern pilgrims – once strangers, now familiar – and seeing the path spill out in front of us, I felt the mixture of pride and purpose that only a pilgrimage can bring.

The long walk

All over the world, faiths of all persuasions put pilgrimage at the heart of their beliefs. A walk to a holy place, whether it's Canterbury Cathedral, the River Ganges, Mecca or Jerusalem, is a vital way to keep beliefs alive and followers engaged. Many of these routes have been walked continually for centuries and have always attracted huge numbers of pilgrims. While some routes are exclusive to that religion, others welcome all comers, who may walk alongside the faithful for their own, secular reasons.

The huge and growing popularity of the Christian pilgrimage to Camino de Santiago in Spain has opened people's eyes to the potential of pilgrimage. Many people who have never considered a walk of this length before, and would not consider themselves religious or even particularly sporty, take to the path, determined to reach the end. Among the many things that pilgrimage provides are an end point, a purpose and a real sense of achievement.

Pilgrimage can also be a time to walk with others, either setting out as a group, or travelling with new people you meet along the way. Like Chaucer's motley bunch setting off from London to visit the shrine of Thomas Becket at Canterbury Cathedral, a group of pilgrims can keep each other's spirits aloft and take the pain out of the walking when things get tough.

Pilgrimages of faith around the world

These are some of the better-known pilgrimages that have been walked for centuries and are at the heart of different faiths. Non-believers and other religions are usually (but not always) welcome. Attracting thousands of people, they generally have an infrastructure of accommodation and clearly marked routes to guide the modern pilgrim.

These lengthy walks, sometimes crossing countries and even mountain ranges, can appear daunting. If you don't have the time or energy to do the entire route in one go, then walk them in stages. You can return year after year or month after month and do them in shorter bursts. Specialist tour operators can also help with accommodation and luggage management to take the sting out of the distance. This list of longer faith pilgrimages is selective: there are, of course, many more criss-crossing countries and continents all over the world.

Camino de Santiago, Spain

What it's all about This is the daddy of all pilgrimages and the one whose growing popularity (300,000 pilgrims in 2017) has inspired the revival of many others. It's not one single route, but a network of several extending across Europe, all of which converge on the Cathedral in Santiago de Compostela and the tomb of apostle and martyr St James the Great. The most popular route is the Camino Francés, which starts at Jean-Pied-du-Port and is 780km long.

Santiago has been a pilgrimage destination since AD 814 when the remains of St James arrived in a boat from Jerusalem. During the Middle Ages, walking to Santiago was as important a pilgrimage as going to Rome and Jerusalem. Pilgrimages declined in the fourteenth century but started to pick up again from the 1970s and 1980s, with numbers increasing year by year ever since.

'Camino', incidentally, means a way, journey, mission, trip or excursion. And the word excursion is from Latin – *ex* is 'out' and *curere* 'to run': you run out of your existing world into something new and adventurous.

When to go If you are looking for a quiet, meditative walk it's best to avoid mid-summer on the more popular routes, as it gets very crowded.

What to expect The Camino Francés gets busy during the summer – around 60 per cent of pilgrims choose it – as does the Camino Portuguese which starts at Porto, but other routes are quieter. Much of the walking on the Camino is on flat, man-made paths and roads and is not that demanding (although it is hard on feet not used to walking for days and weeks at a time – be prepared for blisters). A massive infrastructure of dormitories and restaurants has grown up along the route, catering to ever-increasing numbers of pilgrims. Pilgrims carry a scallop shell and a passport, which is necessary to stay in any of the pilgrim accommodation, and which is stamped at each stop. Any pilgrim who has walked the last 100km of the route and has done so for religious reasons is entitled to a certificate called a Compostela.

Who'll be there People from all walks of life and countries, each with different motivations. While many still make the journey with a religious intent, others walk for more personal reasons or simply as exercise or a 'bucket-list' activity. Meeting other pilgrims along the path and hearing their stories is an important part of the trip and is fostered in the *refugios* – pilgrim accommodation. Many extend the pilgrimage beyond Santiago to Finisterre and Muxia, about 88km further along, to reach the sea.

See santiago-compostela.net

Via Francigena: from Canterbury to Rome (England, France, Switzerland and Italy)

What it's all about This 2083-km pilgrimage, from the burial place of St Thomas Becket in Canterbury Cathedral to the tombs of saints Peter and Paul in Rome, used to be as popular with medieval pilgrims as the Camino de Santiago. Like many of the old pilgrimage routes, it fell out of favour post-Reformation, but fragments of the path remained: enough for the Italian government to restore the Italian leg in 2009 and for the Council of Europe to designate it a Major Cultural Route.

The path follows in the footsteps of Archbishop Sigeric the Serious who, in AD 900, walked from Canterbury to Rome to pick up his official pallium (an ecclesiastical vestment) from the Pope. ('Via Francigena' means 'the road that comes from France'.) Pilgrims pick up a passport from the information desk at Canterbury Cathedral and, like the Camino, get it stamped at points along the route.

When to go The longer, warmer days of summer are best for maximum walking opportunities, but the trail can be walked any time of the year.

What to expect Changing scenery: leaving the North Down Way at Dover, the route crosses the Channel then passes cathedrals and abbeys in Picardy (most medieval pilgrimage routes connected religious settlements rather than towns), follows along rural roads and mule tracks into Switzerland, then continues across the Apennine Mountains and down the Italian peninsula to Rome. Accommodation is not as abundant as on the Camino, but some monasteries are starting to offer places for anyone with a pilgrim's passport. Allow four months or so to walk the whole distance, or walk successive one- or two-week sections as part of a longer project. Some holiday operators offer deals for part of the route, and these include accommodation and bag carrying.

Who'll be there Those who have discovered the Via Francigena as a less-travelled and more scenically varied alternative to the Camino de Santiago. Numbers annually are around 1500 pilgrims. Some medieval pilgrims extended their pilgrimage and continued to Jerusalem, and modern pilgrims have started to follow suit. Read one account of this mighty trek in Guy Stagg's book *The Crossway*.

See viefrancigene.org

St Olav's Way (*Pilegrimsleden*), Sweden and Norway

What it's all about Running from Selånger, on the Baltic Sea in Sweden, to Nidaros Cathedral in Trondheim, on the Altantic Ocean of Norway, this is the most northerly pilgrimage route in the world. It follows the one taken by Olav II Haraldsson, King of Norway (1015–1028) who is credited with bringing Christianity to the country. After he was slain in battle in 1030, miracles became associated with his body, resulting in his canonisation in 1031 and the building of a cathedral over his grave. Pilgrims began to arrive in increasing numbers thereafter, although tailed off when the railways arrived, but the route has now been revived. Viking-era grave mounds can be found along the path, suggesting that it was also walked during the Iron Age, though for what purpose is unknown.

When to go Spring (providing snow doesn't block mountain paths) or June and July, when it is light all day, are the best times to walk. August is good, too, but it gets chilly in the evenings. Temperatures drop further in September (although watching the trees changing colour is glorious), and any time after that is best avoided due to cold temperatures and short days.

What to expect The 564-km path takes pilgrims through the full complement of Scandinavian natural attractions, from deep forests to sacred springs, fjords and lakes to meadows and snow-topped mountains. Like the Camino de Santiago, pilgrims are furnished with a pilgrim's passport that is stamped at certified places along the route, and an 'Olav Letter', a diploma that is given to anyone who has walked at least the last 200km of the Way. It is suggested that pilgrims allow twenty-eight days (20km per day) to walk its entire length. The path is clearly waymarked and there are three pilgrim centres along the route (at the start, the middle and the end). Wild camping (up to two nights) is permitted, so it's possible to pitch a tent by a lake and go for an early morning swim. Otherwise, there is a range of cabins, shelters, hostels and farms to stay in. Unlike other pilgrimage routes, it is essential to book accommodation in advance. The Way splits towards the end, with an option of a coastal path and a 'pilgrim boat' to take you across a fjord to Trondheim.

Who'll be there Marketed as a new, long-distance hiking trail with an interesting history, St Olav's Way is attracting increasing numbers of outdoor adventurers (numbers are up 30 per cent each year), mostly from Germany and the Netherlands. It is, therefore, more of a secular pilgrimage route than a religious one, but no less worthwhile for that. It is a wonderful way to live fully in nature for weeks or months, with all the benefits that brings.

See stolavsleden.com

Croagh Patrick, Near Westport, County Mayo, Ireland

What it's all about Tradition has it that St Patrick, Ireland's patron saint, fasted on the summit of the mountain of Croagh Patrick for forty days in AD 441. Ever since, pilgrims have climbed its stony paths to the summit. The peak, which is 750m high, and known as the Reek, is a distinctive pyramidal shape and made of quartzite: you can see why it is considered sacred. It is thought that pilgrimage here predates Christianity and was originally a ritual associated with the Gaelic agricultural festival of Lughnasadh (1 August), which marks the start of the harvest.

From the top of Croagh Patrick pilgrims appreciate eye-opening views of the Mayo countryside, the distant Nephin Beg range of mountains, and the multiple, pretty, domed islands of Clew Bay (of which there are said to be 365).

The pilgrimage can get very crowded (leading to erosion of the paths) on significant dates, with a constantly moving line of pilgrims making their way to the top and back down again, but it is sociable and friendly and attracts people of all ages keen to participate in the walking and the ritual.

When to go Pilgrims climb the Reek all year round, but certain dates are more significant than others. The last Sunday in July, known as Reek Sunday, attracts around 30,000 pilgrims; the last Friday in July, 'Garland Friday', and 15 August, the Feast of the Assumption of Our Lady into Heaven, are also popular dates. A pilgrimage in the warmer, lighter months is recommended as the combination of cold, wet weather, loose footing on rocky paths and a steep ascent can be hazardous.

What to expect Pilgrims, often walking in groups, can choose from a number of routes, with the most popular being the wide and much-walked Pilgrim Route, which starts at the car park. The first stop is at the statue of St Patrick, which was erected by a local priest in 1928, and where prayers and offerings are made before the climb steepens. The walk to the top takes about two and a half hours. The path goes along the shoulder of the mountain where there is a cairn for pilgrims to stop and pray (and a shop selling snacks should the body as well as the spirit need refreshment), then up a steep path to the top, where a small church (built in 1905) makes a satisfactory end to the pilgrimage. Here Mass is held and confessions are heard. The walk back down to the car park takes about one and a half hours.

Who'll be there Visitors are Irish Catholics in the main, although pilgrims have been known to travel to Croagh Patrick from all over the world. Some walk barefoot or crawl on their knees as a form of penance – the paths are made of scree and loose stone, and the weather is often wet, so this takes some doing. Anyone is welcome to make the ascent, though, and many do so, often.

Word of warning Although it is a popular pilgrimage, don't be fooled: the loose stones underfoot, steep climb and danger of inclement weather mean it can also be dangerous. Proper walking boots, waterproofs and a bottle of water are a must.

Further information The Croagh Patrick Visitor Centre is at the base of the mountain at the rear of the car park.

See croagh-patrick.com.

The Hajj, Mecca, Saudi Arabia

What it's all about Every Muslim must make at least one pilgrimage to Mecca, if they can afford to do so and are able bodied. This is called Hajj and is the fifth and final pillar of Islam. The Prophet Muhammad was born in Mecca and it is where he received the first revelation of the Qur'an. During

Hajj, pilgrims pray before the Kaaba ('House of God'), a sacred building originally built, legend has it, by the Prophet Ibrahim and his son Is'mail, as instructed by Allah. The Kaaba is a large black cube-shaped building and Islam's holiest shrine.

When to go Hajj takes place once a year during the twelfth month of the Islamic lunar calendar Dhul-Hijjah, and lasts for five days.

What goes on A way to get closer to Allah, and to connect with Muslims from all over the world, Hajj involves a sequence of rites and rituals. These include walking counterclockwise around the Kaaba seven times, running between the hills of Safa and Marwah, sipping water from the sacred Zamzam Well and throwing stones at the Devil, represented by three pillars.

Who'll be there Millions of Muslims from all over the world: in 2017, a total of 2,352,122 people attended. All are dressed in simple white clothing, called Ihram, which are worn to show that everyone is equal in the eyes of Allah. No non-Muslims are allowed to enter Mecca or to undertake Hajj.

Kumbh Mela, India

What it's all about Hindu myth has it that the gods once fought demons over a pitcher containing *amrita* (nectar) which was believed to bring immortality. During the battle, four drops were spilt onto four cities – Allahabad, Nasik, Haridwar and Ujjain. These cities now hold the Kumbh Mela festival on a rotational basis. ('Mela' means festival and 'kumbh' means pitcher.) Bathing at the confluence of the rivers Ganges, Yamuna and the mystical Saraswati at the most auspicious time is of prime importance and central to the festival. Hindus believe it will free them from the cycle of life and rebirth and cleanse them from sin.

When to go The Kumbh Mela is held once every three years and lasts for fifty-five days. Once every twelve years it becomes even bigger – the Maha Kumbh Mela is the biggest gathering of humanity in the world.

What to expect A colourful and chaotic mass of people will be milling about and bathing in the river.

Who'll be there Many millions of Hindus attend, observed by considerable numbers of tourists. Holy men (*sadhus*) of various sects, either naked or dressed in orange and smeared with ash, are everywhere meditating or practising yoga. Pilgrims come to listen to these men to gain spiritual enlightenment.

Shrine of Our Lady of Guadalupe, Mexico City, Mexico

What it's all about On 12 December 1531 Juan Diego Cuauhtlatoatzin, a poor farmer, saw a vision of the Virgin Mary on Tepeyac Hill, near what is now Mexico City. Speaking to him in his native Aztec tongue, she asked for a church to be built in her honour on the site. Juan Diego told the Catholic bishop what she had said, but he wasn't convinced and asked for a sign. Juan Diego returned to the same place, and this time Mary told him to gather roses growing nearby in his *tilma* (cloak), even though no such flower bloomed in Mexico. When the bishop saw the cloak it was imprinted with Mary's image. This miracle clinched it for the bishop who then used it as a way to convert native people to Catholicism. A church was built, quickly drew pilgrims and is now one of the most visited holy sites in the world.

When to go To get the full flavour of the colourful celebrations, go on 12 December, the anniversary of Juan Diego's vision and the feast day of the Virgin of Gaudalupe.

What to expect Many people are there attending Mass in one of the two basilicas and climbing the hill to the scene of the vision. The Pilgrim's Path will take you to the top where there is a small church. Juan Diego's *tilma* is housed in the Minor Basilica of Our Lady of Guadalupe in a gilded frame behind the altar and is one of the most visited Catholic pilgrimage sites in the world.

Who'll be there Mexican Catholics mostly. Veneration of Our Lady of Guadalupe is widespread in the country and this is the place to honour her.

Interesting footnote Juan Diego became the first Roman Catholic indigenous saint when he was canonised in 2002.

See basilica.mxv.mx

Six British pilgrimage routes

As more of us modern pilgrims pull on our boots and step outdoors, more paths open up. The growing popularity of pilgrimage has meant that in Britain several new pilgrimage routes have been devised. These incorporate medieval paths and practices with the addition of modern mapping, GPS routes and helpful websites. Well-marked, they criss-cross the country from north to south and are an excellent way of exploring the country while practising pilgrimage.

St Cuthbert's Way: from Melrose (Scotland) to Lindisfarne (Northumberland)

This 100-km pilgrimage follows the path taken by seventh-century monk, bishop and hermit Cuthbert from Melrose Abbey in Scotland across the border to Lindisfarne on the Northumberland coast. It is a glorious walk through the Cheviot hills to the coast and ends in spectacular fashion with a walk across a causeway (called the Pilgrim's Path) to the tidal island of Lindisfarne (tides permitting).

Cuthbert was a medieval monk, bishop and, latterly, hermit, who led an exemplary holy life embracing good works and austerity. He became hugely important after his death when his body was exhumed and found to be perfectly preserved. Although he died in a simple cell on the island of Inner Farne, the monks of Lindisfarne fled with his coffin during invasion by the Vikings (they also took the Lindisfarne Gospels). After seven years of travelling, they settled in Durham, where Cuthbert's tomb became the seed that grew into the mighty Durham Cathedral (see page 158), a great centre of pilgrimage throughout the Middle Ages.

See stcuthbertsway.info

An alternative pilgrimage to Lindisfarne The Northern Cross Pilgrimage, which takes place during the week before Easter, starts at different locations and ends at Holy Island. Christian pilgrims walk between 70 and 120 miles carrying a cross.

See Northerncross.co.uk

North Wales Pilgrim's Way (Taith Pererin Gogledd Cymru): from Holywell to Bardsey Island

During the Middle Ages, three pilgrimages to Bardsey Island, off the tip of the Llyn Peninsula in North Wales, were the equivalent of one to Rome. A sacred place worth reaching, it was said that 20,000 saints were buried there. In 2001, a 222-km route from Holywell, in Flintshire, to Bardsey was created for modern pilgrims, replicating the medieval path. It takes its inspiration from two Welsh saints: Winefride (whose well is at Holywell, see page 48) and her uncle Beuno, linking the places associated with them. The route, which is divided into twenty-five sections of 4km to 19km, takes between ten and fifteen days depending on your pace.

The Llyn Peninsula is a wild and lovely spot, and the pilgrimage path goes through woods, rivers and mountains, passing a Celtic cross and a stone circle, then along the coast. The final leg is by boat across the whirlpools and currents of the Sound to Bardsey Island itself – a short ride over the water to a different world.

See pilgrims-way-north-wales.org

St Peter's Way, Essex

The small and ancient (660–662) Chapel of St Peter-on-the-Wall is one of the oldest in Britain. It stands alone and quiet on the Dengie Peninsula in Essex, overlooking the saltmarsh and the sea. It was used as a barn for centuries until it was restored in 1920. Since then it has been used for regular services, including those by the nearby Christian-based Othona Community.

The 66-km St Peter's Way starts at Chipping Ongar and ends at this lovely place, taking four days at a steady pace. The pilgrimage crosses wide-open farmland and a bird-rich reservoir, running alongside the Blackwater estuary before approaching St Peter's along the sea wall.

On the first Saturday of July, a group following a mini pilgrimage that has attracted 1500 people in the past leaves St Thomas Church in Bradwell and walks through the fields to St Peter's Chapel – a distance of about two miles. On arrival, other attractions like story-telling and music are laid on as part of the Bradwell Gathering, a celebration of this special place.

See ldwa.org.uk; bradwellchapel.org

Two Saints Way: Chester to Lichfield

This new 148-km pilgrimage route, which had its inaugural walk in 2012, links two important medieval cathedrals – Chester and Lichfield – and their relevant saints, Chad and Werburgh. It includes nods to medieval pilgrimage practices – modern pilgrims can leave a stone in St Michael and St Wulfad's Church in the village of Stone along the way, and are encouraged to mark a cross on their forearm like their medieval forebears. The route is divided into four sections. Waymarked in one direction with the cross of St Chad and with the goose of St Werburgh in the other, it passes alongside canals, across fields and by hill forts and Celtic crosses.

See twosaintsway.org.uk

Cornish Celtic Way: from St Germans to St Michael's Mount

This new pilgrimage route of 201km incorporates two older ones: The Saints' Way (from Padstow to Fowey) and St Michael's Way (from Lelant to St Michael's Mount). Zig-zagging Cornwall from south to north and back again, and including 96km of coastal paths, the entire walk takes around two weeks. It's divided into sixteen sections, though, so can be completed over months or even years. The organisers' aim is that modern pilgrims 'develop spiritual growth and personal reflection' through stories of the Celtic saints who brought Christianity to Cornwall between AD 500 and 600. The route knits together many ancient and Celtic sights including holy wells, standing stones and churches, plus an awful lot of spectacular scenery. (For more on St Michael's Way, see page 56.)

See cornishcelticway.co.uk

The Holy Mile: Walsingham, Norfolk

During the Middle Ages, Walsingham was second only to Canterbury in ranks of English pilgrimage. The Shrine of Our Lady was established in 1061 when a Saxon noblewoman called Richeldis de Faverches had a vision: she was told by the Virgin Mary to build a replica of the Holy House in Nazareth as a reminder of the Annunciation. This she duly did and the shrine, with its relic of a phial of the Virgin's milk, drew a steady stream of pilgrims.

During the Reformation in 1538 the shrine was destroyed and the statue of the Virgin Mary was burnt. All was quiet until 1896, when Charlotte Pearson Boyd bought a fourteenth-century wayside chapel near the hamlet of Houghton St Giles. The chapel had once been the last on the route to Walsingham and she restored it for Catholic use. Since 1897 it has steadily received pilgrims, and these days attracts around 150,000 a year from all over the world, including thousands of Catholic Tamils from Sri Lanka in May and July. The mile between the chapel and Walsingham itself is called the Holy Mile and is walked barefoot by many pilgrims.

A mindful pilgrimage with other people

Going on a pilgrimage with other people, or to a place where others are gathered, is quite a different experience to walking alone or with a single companion. While they can be sociable and supportive experiences, group pilgrimages make it easy to get distracted and lose sight of why you are there: chatting to your fellow pilgrims can make the miles pass pleasingly, but it takes your mind away from your surroundings and the here and now. You become less mindful. A different mindset is needed, one that isn't anti-social but that ensures that you stay in the present.

Here are some thoughts:

- Suggest to the group (or to the leader of the group) that some time during the day be spent in silence. This could be in the morning when you set off and no one feels sociable anyway. A period of half an hour walking quietly together will focus your mind on your intention and keep you centred.

- If you find yourself walking in a particularly lovely or spiritually uplifting place and everyone is talking, marching along and not noticing, call a halt to the pilgrimage and suggest they look around. They will thank you for it and you will be able to pause and have a moment to enjoy the experience.

- Respond to the experience and to your surroundings creatively. Stopping to sketch something that catches your eye, or to jot down some thoughts in a notebook, takes you out of the group dynamic and into your own space. It will also help you to stay mindful and to remember the experience. One way to do this is to write a haiku. These short poems, invented within the Japanese Zen tradition, get right to the heart of things. Written in just three lines of seventeen syllables, which follow a five, seven, five pattern, they look deceptively simple. Writing them requires some skill and thought, but is well worth the effort.

  Here's an example written by Matsuo Basho (1644–1694), who was considered the greatest haiku poet: 'Autumn moonlight – / a worm digs silently / into the chestnut.' And another by a more modern master of the haiku, Masaoka Shiki (1867–1902): 'The summer river: / although there is a bridge, my horse / goes through the water.'

12

The Modern Pilgrim's Guide to Useful Stuff

Before you set out on a pilgrimage, there are a few things to consider. Not just the route, but what to take, where to stay and, most importantly, your reason for going. Here are some guidelines which may help.

Pilgrims' practical pointers

Be clear about your purpose Are you going because you are at a crossroads in your life and need space to think? Do you just want to get away for a few days and get outdoors and into nature? Or do you want to strengthen your faith? Whatever the reason, keep it in mind before you set off. It will keep you focused and mindful.

Be aware of the route Don't rely exclusively on waymarks and a 'good sense of direction': a slight deviation from your route can send you miles off course. Take a map or download a GPS app with the route ready loaded (britishpilgrimage.org/finding-your-way has good intelligence on this).

Be contactable Keep your phone charged in case you get lost or need help. Carry a portable battery charger for this purpose.

Be hydrated Carry a bottle of water in your rucksack and sip from it frequently. Steady fluid intake to keep hydrated is better than waiting until you are parched and gulping huge quantities. Be wary of drinking from streams: water is best filtered first to be on the safe side. A Lifestraw bottle (lifestraw. com) makes contaminated water safe to drink and is light to carry and easy to use.

Be well shod Make sure your boots or shoes are comfortable, waterproof and robust. Boots that offer ankle protection are preferable, especially when walking over scree, slippery surfaces, or going downhill. Good-quality walking socks are also recommended and help prevent blisters. Take Compeed plasters in case blisters do appear, and try to resist popping them.

Behave Remember to ask permission to visit sites on private land – many Neolithic long barrows or standing stones are in the middle of agricultural fields. Don't get carried away when you arrive: not everyone appreciates drumming, dancing and/ or chanting. Respect the sacredness of the place and the land on which it stands.

Be tidy Remember the foremost rule of walking in the wild – leave no trace. Even better, pick up any bits of litter you find and dispose of it in the proper place.

What to take

One of the joys of a pilgrimage is that you travel light. The fewer things you carry, the lighter will be your load and the greater the spring in your step. As well as a waterproof jacket and trousers, a good pair of boots and socks, there are one or two other things that will help you along the way. These are some of the items recommended on the Camino de Santiago website (santiago-compostela.net) and are worth considering for any long pilgrimage. Whatever you take, keep it as minimal as possible. The weight of what you carry in your rucksack will have a direct impact on the benefits of your pilgrimage. Water is often the heaviest item, so remember to factor its weight, and that of any snacks, into your packing.

Sleeping bag This is vital if staying in dormitories.
Headtorch Have one handy to illuminate the path as light fades.
Toilet roll Take out the centre and flatten it to reduce its bulk.
A scarf A small, light and useful piece of fabric that can be used for many different purposes, from preventing sunburn on necks, to a cleaning cloth, a table cloth and a bandana.
A few items of clothing that can be handwashed and worn on rotation This means you won't need so many.
Plastic bags Protect your belongings, especially anything electronic, from rain.

The pilgrim's staff

The wooden staff is, alongside the scallop shell, the most recognisable symbol of a pilgrim. In the Middle Ages it was a useful tool for keeping wild animals at bay, beating back undergrowth and walloping any assailants. Whereas these eventualities are unlikely to befall the modern pilgrim, it is still a useful prop to carry. Like a rustic version of a Nordic pole, it will help you over rough and hilly terrain and take the pressure off your knees. It can be used to probe and prod anything unknown or suspicious and will help you dislodge an apple from a high branch or fish lost belongings from a lake. A staff may feel a little conspicuous for a city pilgrimage but out in the country it will elevate you beyond a mere rambler. You will become a walker with a purpose.

When fashioning a staff, make it long enough to grab the top easily at shoulder height. If it ends with a short fork, so much the better: then you have a natural place to rest your thumb. It should be cut from a tree that is grown sustainably, and preferably has some folklore-ish associations for extra resonance. Coppiced trees (which are cut back to ground level to encourage growth), such as hazel or willow, fit the bill nicely as they have multiple, flexible, straight stems. Hazel is supposed to protect against evil sprites, its thinner branches are used to dowse for water, and its nuts were once carried as charms to ward off rheumatism – all handy attributes to have on a pilgrimage. Willow's ability to regrow speedily has come to symbolise renewal, growth and vitality, also useful qualities to have on board. Both will produce a staff that will become your constant and sturdy companion as you make you way along the path.

The Countryside Code

Be safe. Plan ahead and follow any signs.

Leave gates and property as you find them.

Protect plants and animals, and take your litter home.

Keep dogs under close control.

Consider other people.

The journey home

Coming home is as much a part of pilgrimage as leaving. Without the knowledge that there is a familiar place to return to when the walking is over, a pilgrim becomes a rootless nomad. And while spending time away from the familiarities and concerns of daily life is liberating and generally pretty wonderful, putting the key in your own front door is a sure way to elicit a sigh of contentment.

The return home is also the time to reflect on what you experienced on your pilgrimage. Rather than rushing straight back into the hurly-burly and demands of work, family and friends, take a little time to settle. After you've unpacked your rucksack, had a bath and a cup of tea, think about where you have walked and what it has meant to you. Capturing these thoughts in a notebook, or by uploading photographs from your phone to your computer, will help to fix them in your mind and create a place to return to mentally in the future. Then, refreshed and rested, you can re-engage with life and all its demands.

Until, that is, you hear the call of the path again. It will always be there waiting: all you have to do is put on your boots and walk out of the door.

Bibliography

About pilgrimage and walking

A Philosophy of Walking (Verso) Frédéric Gros
The imperative of walking explained through the experiences of writers and philosophers.
The Lost Art of Walking (Harbour) Geoff Nicholson
Personal rambles and hikes provide a platform for musings on the power of pedestrianism.
The Extra Mile: a 21st-century pilgrimage (Continuum)
Peter Stanford
Travels to key sacred sites in search of faith in Britain today.
Wanderlust: a history of walking (Verso) Rebecca Solnit
The cultural significance of walking and how it has shaped us and our surroundings.
Hidden Histories (Frances Lincoln) Mary-Ann Ochota
A guide to reading the British landscape, from Neolithic sites to ancient pathways.
The Art of Wandering: the writer as walker (Oldcastle Books)
Merlin Coverley

A history of the writer as walker, including pilgrims, flaneurs and vagrants.

The Art of Mindful Walking (Leaping Hare) Adam Ford
Musings on pedestrian mindfulness.

The Art of Pilgrimage: the seeker's guide to making travel sacred (Conrari Press) Phil Coisineau
A compendium of stories, quotes and meditative suggestions that take the reader through all the stages of pilgrimage.

Ways to Wander (Triarchy Press) Clare Qualmann and Claire Hind
Fifty-four imaginative and thought-provoking walks suggested by artists.

Ancient paths

The Old Straight Track (Head of Zeus) Alfred Watkins
The Ley Hunter's Manual: a guide to early tracks (Ley Hunter Library) Alfred Watkins
The Old Ways (Penguin) Robert Macfarlane
Leys: secret spirit paths in Ancient Britain (Wooden Books) Danny Sullivan
The Spine of Albion (Sacred Lands Publishing) Gary Biltcliffe and Caroline Hoare
Songlines (Vintage Classics) Bruce Chatwin
Dartmoor Mindscapes: re-visioning a sacred landscape (Stone Seeker) Peter Wright
Holloway (Faber & Faber) Robert Macfarlane, Stanley Donwood and Dan Richards

Water worlds

Sacred Wells: a study in the history, meaning and mythology of holy wells and waters (Algora Publishing) Gary R Varner
The Living Stream: holy wells in historical context (Boydell Press) James Rattue
Sacred Springs: holy wells in Great Britain (Wooden Books) Christina Martin
The Fish Ladder (Bloomsbury) Katharine Norbury
To the River (Canongate) Olivia Laing
Wild Swimming Walks (Wild Things) Kenwood Ladies Pond Association
Wild Swim (Guardian Books) Kate Rew
Wild Swimming: 300 hidden dips in the rivers, lakes and waterfalls of Britain (Wild Things) Daniel Start
Waterlog: a swimmer's journey through Britain (Vintage) Roger Deakin

The mighty mountain

The Living Mountain (Canongate) Nan Shepherd
The Druid Way (Element) Philip Carr-Gomm
Celtic Sacred Landscapes (Thames & Hudson) Nigel Pennick
To a Mountain in Tibet (Vintage) Colin Thubron

The wisdom of trees

Aboreal, a collection of new woodland writing (Commonground)
Gossip from the Forest (Granta) Sara Maitland

Wildwood: a journey through trees (Penguin) Roger Deakin
Out of the Woods: the armchair guide to trees (Short Books) Will Cohu
The Long, Long Life of Trees (Yale) Fiona Stafford
The Tree Climber's Guide (HarperCollins) Jack Cooke
Meetings with Remarkable Trees (Cassell) Thomas Pakenham

Gardens for the soul

The Garden Awakening: designs to nurture our land and ourselves (Green Books) Mary Reynolds
Japanese Gardens (Taschen) Gunther Nitschke
Cultivating Sacred Space: gardening for the soul (Pomegranate) Elizabeth Murray
Paradise Gardens: the world's most beautiful Islamic gardens (Two Roads) Monty Don
Sacred Geography (Gaia) Paul Devereux

Following the labyrinth

Mazes and Labyrinths in Great Britain (Wooden Books) John Martineau
Labyrinths: ancient myths and modern uses (Gothic Image) Sig Lonegren
Magical Paths: mazes and labyrinths in the 21st century (Mitchell Beazley) Jeff Saward
Red Thread: on mazes and labyrinths (Jonathan Cape) Charlotte Higgins

Icons and idols

The Green Man (Shire Library) Richard Hayman
The Quest for the Green Man (Godsfield) John Matthews
A Little Book of the Green Man (Aurum Press) Mike Harding
Sheela-Na-Gigs: origins and functions (National Museum of Ireland) Eamonn P Kelly

Temples

The Temple, meeting place of heaven and earth (Thames & Hudson) John M Lundquist
Sacred Geography: deciphering hidden codes in the landscape (Gaia) Paul Devereux
The Sacred Place (Cassell & Co) Paul Devereux
The Modern Antiquarian (Thorsons) Julian Cope
Rings of Stone: the prehistoric stone circles of Britain and Ireland (Book Club Associates) Aubrey Burl
Mysterious Britain (Paladin) Janet and Colin Bord
The Traveller's Key to Sacred England (Harrap Columbus) John Michell

In the city

Lunch Poems (City Lights) Frank O'Hara
Flaneuse: women walk the city in Paris, New York, Tokyo, Venice and London (Vintage) Lauren Elkin
Psychogeography (Pocket Essentials) Merlin Coverley
Mrs Dalloway (Wordsworth Editions) Virginia Woolf

Following in the footsteps

M Train (Bloomsbury) Patti Smith
Footsteps: literary pilgrimages around the world (Three Rivers Press) The New York Times

Faith routes

The Crossway (Picador) Guy Stagg
Lightfoot Guide to the Via Francigena (Pilgrimage Publications) Paul Chinn and Babette Gallard
Spanish Steps: travels with my donkey (Vintage) Tim Moore

Useful websites and organisations

The Ancient Yew Group: ancient-yew.org
British Camino: caminouk.com
British Pilgrimage Trust: britishpilgrimage.org
Buxton Well Dressing: buxtonwelldressing.co.uk
The Chalice Well: chalicewell.org.uk
The Findhorn Foundation: findhorn.org
Friends of the Dymock Poets: dymockpoets.org.uk
The Gatekeeper Trust: gatekeeper.org.uk
Green Pilgrimage: greenpilgrimageeurope.net
The island of Iona: welcometoiona.com
The Labyrinth Society: labyrinthsociety.org
Lourdes: lourdes-france.org
Mandy Pullen, shamanic practitioner: mandypullen.co.uk
The Megalithic Portal: megalithic.co.uk
The Order of Bards Ovates and Druids: druidry.org

The Outdoor Swimming Society: outdoorswimmingsociety.com
The Pilgrim's Way: pilgrimswaycanterbury.org
River and Lake Swimming Association: river-swimming.co.uk
Saffron Walden Maze Festival: saffronwaldenmazefestival.co.uk
Woodland Trust: woodlandtrust.org.uk

A few films to inspire

The Way A father continues the journey along the Camino de Santiago started by his son who died on the path.
Wild: a journey from lost to found Based on the true story of Cheryl Strayed who walked the Pacific Coast Trail alone following the death of her mother and end of her marriage.
Walking the Camino: six ways to Santiago Six different pilgrims with six different reasons to walk the Camino.
Peace Walker Inspired by the life of a Peace Pilgrim who left home one day to walk for peace and never stopped.
Walkabout A brother and sister left in the desert following their father's death meet an Aboriginal boy on his Walkabout rite of passage.
A Walk in the Woods Based on Bill Bryson's account of his hike along the Appalachian Trail with a friend.
Tracks One girl's nine-month journey across the Australian desert with her dog and four camels.

Acknowledgements

Thanks to the following fellow pilgrims for their inspiration and companionship: Debi Angel, Max Bell, Edwina Biucchi, Carolyn Boyd, Vanessa Easlea, Siân Evans, Sarah Evans, David Furlong and Fiona Hopes (The Gatekeeper Trust), Jane Graham-Maw, John Gogerty (big footsteps to follow), Peter Knight, Liz Macdonald, Will Parsons and Guy Hayward (The British Pilgrimage Trust), Mandy Pullen, Jackie Swanson, The Trotters (Sally Byford, Cate Daniel, Catherine Fleming), Peter Vallance, Sue Wallace.

Index